KARNATAKA PANCHAYAT ELECTIONS 1995

Process, Issues and Membership Profile

Karnataka Panchayat Elections 1995

Process, Issues and Membership Profile

K. Subha

Published for

INSTITUTE OF SOCIAL SCIENCES

by

CONCEPT PUBLISHING COMPANY, NEW DELHI 110 059

The two research projects: 'Election Process and Issues: Karnataka Panchayat Elections 1995' and 'Social Background of Elected Representatives of Gram, Taluk and Zilla Panchayats 1995' and this publication were made possible by grants from:

The Department of Rural Development and Panchayat Raj,
Government of Karnataka
and
The Ford Foundation

ISBN 81-7022-612-0

First Published 1997

Published and Printed by
Ashok Kumar Mittal
Concept Publishing Company
A/15-16, Commercial Block, Mohan Garden
NEW DELHI 110 059 (India)

Layout by
Institute of Social Sciences
B-7/18 Safdarjung Enclave
New Delhi 110 029

Foreword

The Institute of Social Sciences has been keeping an abiding interest in the Panchayati Raj experiments taking place in Karnataka. It was at the initiative of the Institute, a national seminar was organised in New Delhi in 1985 to bring on the national agenda the new panchayati raj system which was being inaugurated in the state. Since then several valuable studies on the subject have been undertaken by the Institute which have become a rich source material for panchayat representatives, functionaries and scholars.

When the March 1995 panchayat elections were announced the Institute was keen to study the panchayat election process and issues as well as the social background of elected members. Not only the zilla panchayat and taluk panchayat elections of 1995 but the gram panchayat elections of 1993 were included in a project submitted to the Department of Rural Development and Panchayati Raj in June 1995. Mr. M. P. Prakash, the Honourable Minister for Rural Development and Panchayati Raj, Government of Karnataka, and Principal Secretary of the Department Mr. S. S. Meenakshisundaram evinced keen interest in this project. It was sanctioned on January 9, 1996.

The Institute conducted the field work for four months. All the districts in Karnataka were included in the sample survey to widen the prospects of the study. A total of 3,343 people were interviewed for election process study and 4,775 elected representatives were interviewed to understand the social background of the emerging leadership. The data for this work was collected by following field investigators:

1. Mr. Ananda. N.
2. Mr. G. M. David.
3. Mr. Girish N. V.
4. Mr. Gopala Krishna. C.
5. Ms. Haleema. K.
6. Ms. Harini. N.
7. Mr. Harish. M. S.
8. Ms. Jayashree. M. B.
9. Mr. Kiran Kumar. B. P.
10. Mr. Peerappa. L.
11. Mr. Ravi. B. S.
12. Ms. Rosa. P. M.

13. Ms. Rukimini. K.
14. Mr. Shadakshariah. D.
15. Ms. Shakuntala. M. D.
16. Ms. Savitri. S. P.
17. Mr. Sridhara Babu. M. N
18. Mr. Srinivasa. A.
19. Mr. Thandava Murthy. K. N

This study is a sequel to our earlier studies of 1987 elections and elected representatives. The interim findings were released to the press on December 8, 1995, which were highly appreciated by the public.

The Institute is deeply grateful to C. Narayanaswamy, Member of Parliament from Bangalore North who was the former chairperson of Bangalore Rural Zilla Parishad for going through the report and tables meticulously and giving valuable suggestions for improvement.

Mr. David D. Arnold (Representative) and Mr. Terrence George (Programme Officer) of the Ford Foundation extended the necessary support and encouraged us at every step of this study.

Our Southern Regional office at Bangalore did an excellent job in executing this project. Dr. K. Subha, Regional Coordinator (South), ISS, coordinated the study ably assisted by Mr. K. K. Bhavanishankar. This publication will be a source book for the elected representatives, researchers as well as for the panchayat training programmes all over the country.

Institute of Social Sciences
New Delhi
1 September 1996

GEORGE MATHEW
Director

Contents

List of Tables

Chapter I

Introduction

George Mathew

India has a long tradition of local self-government. Going back more than 4,000 years, this institution has survived numerous political changes and upheavals in the ancient and medieval periods till the advent of the British. With colonial administration, the pattern and working of the local bodies have undergone marked changes.

One of the regions where local self-government was strong was Mysore (now Karnataka). Inscriptions dating back to 1005 AD provide considerable information on the subject. The tradition of village bodies was very strong. In *agrahara* villages, the assembly of the *mahajans* (heads of families of scholarly Brahmins) served as the local body. At times the village assembly was known by a numerical suffix as in the case of *aivattu okkalu* (50 families) or *muvattu okkalu* (30 families). The functions of the village assembly included building and maintaining temples, arranging festivals and *jatras*, running choultries (Kannada term for charity homes) and *aravattiges* (centres to distribute water), collecting tolls, conferring gifts for meritorious service, installing hero-statues (for heroes who die in village defence during raids by enemies or bandits), maintaining the family of such deceased heroes by grant of land and settling disputes. A record from Sorab taluk speaks of the whole assembly of a village functioning as *dharmadhyaksha* (judge) in settling a land dispute. The assembly could also outlaw a person or ostracise him.

The assemblies flourished under the Vijayanagara empire and even under the Muslim rulers. However, the colonial period marked a radical departure in every aspect. As the British consolidated their rule, they introduced and developed their own brand of local government.

Constitution of a local fund for the construction of roads and other subsidiary works, and establishment of local fund committees in each district in 1874 marked the beginning of modern local government system in the state. However, these committees were subordinate to the bureaucracy and membership was almost entirely restricted to officials. Hence they did not evoke local interest and initiative. The Mysore Local Boards Act of 1902 was a step forward. It provided for a three-tier local self-government consisting of union (village) panchayats with a nominated Chairman, a taluk board with a sub-divisional officer as President, and a district board with a Deputy Commissioner as President.

In 1914, the government of Mysore constituted two committees: (i) the Local Self-Government Committee with M. Kantharaj Urs as Chairman, and (ii) the Local Finance Committee presided over by Dewan Bahadur C. Srinivasa Iyengar. These committees went into the question of liberalising the constitution and powers of local bodies to make them effective. They recommended an elected majority in all districts and taluk boards, that is, local boards and independent powers for the taluk boards. The Local Boards and Village Panchayats Act VI of 1918 provided for the establishment of village panchayats with enhanced powers and participation by elected members. This was the first significant step in establishing separate self-government bodies for rural areas in the state.

Between 1919 and 1948, 20 native states passed acts for the establishment of panchayats as local self governing bodies along democratic lines. Mysore state was one among 20 when it enacted in 1926 the Mysore District and Mysore Village Panchayats Act. It provided the district boards and the village panchayats with adequate powers, functions and resources. The Act abolished taluk boards from the local self-government system which continued till 1959. In Coorg, there were only village panchayats established in 1926 under the Coorg Village Panchayat Act.

In the wake of Independence, the trend was towards making local bodies autonomous and hence effective. Mahatma Gandhi's idea of *gram swaraj* articulated this concern. He preached a new philosophy of 'ruralism' because India was largely rural and, according to Gandhiji villages should govern themselves through elected panchayats to become self-sufficient. Gandhiji's ideas had a profound impact on the society and politics of Karnataka.

When the Community Development Programme started nationwide in 1952, Karnataka (then Mysore state) implemented it earnestly. But it could not deliver much. As the Balwantrai Mehta Committee observed, the main factor responsible for the failure of the Community Development Programme was the absence of people's participation.

It may be mentioned here that the new state of Mysore (later Karnataka) inherited in 1956 varying patterns of local government from its five integrating areas (Mysore, Madras, Bombay, Hyderabad and Coorg).

Following the recommendation of the Balwantrai Mehta Committee, Karnataka created a three-tier system of panchayati raj as the institutional arrangement to make people's participation meaningful and effective. With the passing of the Mysore Village Panchayats and Local Boards Act 1959, panchayats became a system of local self-government equipped to perform developmental, administrative and political tasks.

The three tiers in the panchayat structure were: village panchayat/town panchayat (VP/TP) at the village level, taluk development board (TDB) at the taluk level, and district development council (DDC) at the district level. VPs/TPs and TDBs were directly elected tiers, while DDC was mainly a bureaucratic tier. In 1983, on the expiry of the term of the panchayats, administrators were appointed by the government.

The year 1983 was a watershed in the history of panchayati raj in Karnataka. For the first time Congress Party lost power in the state and the Janata Party formed the government. One of the election planks of the Janata Party was the reinvigoration and revitalisation of panchayati raj institutions to enable them to play a more effective role in the process of rural development. In order to fulfil its election promise, the Janata government introduced a bill, patterned on the recommendations of the Asoka Mehta Committee, in the state assembly in August 1983. It was subsequently referred to a Joint Select Committee of the legislature. It got the assent of the President of India in July 1985. The Act was known as the Karnataka Zilla Parishads, Taluk Panchayat Samitis, Mandal Panchayats and Nyaya Panchayats Act 1983.

According to Section 271 (5) of the 1983 Act when a mandal panchayat or zilla parishad is dissolved, it shall be reconstituted in the manner provided in this Act before the end of six months from the date of such dissolution. The Act of 1959 did not contain such a provision with the result many dissolved panchayats did not have elections for months together, and administrators appointed by the government continued to administer.

A significant feature of the 1983 Act was that it made up to 25 per cent provision for women members, including SC and ST women, in local bodies.

In addition to the zilla parishad at the district level and the mandal panchayat comprising of a group of villages, the Act also provided for two other statutory bodies – the taluk panchayat samiti at the taluk/block level, which is an advisory and coordinating body with no separate planning and executive powers, and the gram sabha (village assembly). The mandal panchayat was envisaged as the first elected tier located between the village and the taluk, while the zilla parishad as the second directly elected tier was a powerful body which administered schemes and programmes evolved by it and transferred by the government to it.

Women in large numbers were expected to enter the political arena which hitherto had been the exclusive preserve of men. Earlier, very few women members could be co-opted by the taluk panchayat samitis or nominated to the mandal panchayats by the respective zilla parishads, if they so desired.

The government had lowered the voting age to 18. Elections were held on 12 January 1987 for 887 seats in 19 zilla parishads, and on 20 January for nearly 55,000 seats in 2,465 mandals. The Janata Party bagged 448 seats to gain control of eleven zilla parishads directly and five with the help of its legislators as ex-officio members. The Congress (I) won 393 seats to gain control of two zilla parishads on its own and one with the help of its legislators.

In the mandal panchayat elections the Janata Party won 27,353 seats and 1,311 mandals while Congress (I) came second with 20,679 seats and 689 mandals. In the other mandals no party gained a majority.

The 1983 Act ushered in decentralisation to an unprecedented degree and the newly elected representatives took office shortly after the elections but their first financial year started with 1 April, 1987. They held office till early 1992.

Empirical studies have shown that the Act was able to initiate changes in the panchayati raj functioning. However, it could not substantially alter the panchayat leadership or the rural power structure. The system remained more or less the domain of upper-income, landowning and dominant caste members.

The Congress (I) came to power in the 1989 assembly elections. The first five-year term of the zilla parishads elected in 1987 came to an end in the second week of January 1992. Instead of holding elections, administrators were appointed by the Congress government to zilla parishads and mandal panchayats. A new bill was introduced by the government in the Legislative Assembly on 1 April 1993 consequent upon the changes proposed in the Constitution (Seventy-third Amendment) Act 1992. It was passed on 7 April. The Legislative Council unanimously passed the bill on 13 April and it came into force from 18 May 1993. Thus the Karnataka

Panchayati Raj Act 1993 replaced the Karnataka Zilla Parishads, Taluk Panchayat Samithis, Mandal Panchayats and Nyaya Panchayats Act 1983.

The 1993 Karnataka Panchayat Raj Act was severely criticised. Those opposed to it pointed out that the 1983 Act was far more committed to the ethos of democratic decentralisation than the 1993 Act. However, the supporters of the new Act highlighted the reservation of seats for the socially weaker groups and women and the inclusion of many activities related to local development and natural resource management as welcome features.

The Act established a three-tier panchayat raj system in the state with elected bodies at gram, taluk and district levels 'for greater participation of the people and more effective implementation of rural development programmes in the state.'

The following were the salient features of the Act:

1 It established a three-tier panchayat system in the state based on the population as ascertained at the preceding census of which the figures have been published. It envisaged elected bodies at all the three levels.

2. It provided for reservation of seats in favour of Scheduled Castes and Scheduled Tribes in proportion to their population, and for reservation of not less than one-third of the total seats for women at all levels.

3. It also provided for reservation of one-third of the total seats at all levels for the persons belonging to Backward Classes with an annual income below Rs. 10,000.

4. Offices of chairpersons at all levels were also reserved in favour of Scheduled Castes, Scheduled Tribes and Backward Classes, with women getting not less than one-third in the reserved and unreserved categories of offices of adhyakshas and upadhyakshas

5. It envisaged the constitution of a state election commission, the state finance commission and district planning committee.

THE THREE-TIER PANCHAYATI RAJ SYSTEM

Gram Panchayat

According to the Act, normally a gram panchayat will be constituted for a population between 3,000 and 5,000. The area covered by a gram panchayat will consist of a village or a group of villages. There will be one member for every 400 persons.

The adhyaksha and upadhyaksha (president and vice-president) are to be elected from among the elected members.

There are three standing committees, namely:

1. Production Committee
2. Social Justice Committee
3. Amenities Committee

A secretary is appointed by the government as the administrative head of the gram panchayat.

The main functions of the gram panchayat are to promote economic and social welfare, education and health. Under the Act, the state government gives an annual grant of Rs. 1.25 lakh per panchayat apart from release of grants under various plan schemes.

Taluk Panchayat

For each taluk there shall be a taluk panchayat consisting of local representatives from the state legislature and Parliament, one-fifth of the gram panchayat adhyakshas in the taluk chosen by lots every year (in rotation). Members are directly elected from separate territorial constituencies at the rate of one member for every 10,000 population.

The elected members of the taluk panchayat have to choose two members from among themselves to be the adhyaksha and upadhyaksha. The taluk panchayat will have the following standing committees.

1. General Standing Committee
2. Finance, Audit and Planning Committee
3. Social Justice Committee

A Group-A officer of the state civil services is to be the administrative head of the taluk panchayat.

Taluk panchayats are empowered to supervise the activities of gram panchayats in their jurisdiction.

Zilla Panchayat

Each district will have a zilla panchayat consisting of the members of Parliament and state legislature from within the district, the adhyakshas of taluk panchayats in the district, and elected members in accordance with the scale of one member for 40,000 of the population.

The elected members shall choose two members from amongst them to be adhyaksha and upadhyaksha. The zilla panchayat will have the following standing committees:

1. General Standing Committee
2. Finance, Audit and Planning Committee
3. Social Justice Committee
4. Education and Health Committee
5. Agriculture and Industries Committee

The chief executive officer, not below the rank of deputy commissioner, is to be the administrative head of the zilla panchayat. The Act reduced the powers of the zilla panchayat substantially. The chief executive officer was not under the adhyaksha. He had the power to assign duties and supervise zilla panchayat officials in accordance with the rules made by the state government. He was to report directly to the government.

The adhyaksha is to merely convene, preside over and conduct meetings.

It may be noted here that the Janata Dal government through an ordinance made adhyakshas of zilla and taluka panchayats executive heads and gave them executive powers. The functioning of chief executive officers was made subject to the general power of superintendence and control of zilla panchayat and taluk panchayat presidents.

Gram Sabha

The gram sabha is a statutory body today. It is obligatory on the part of the gram panchayat to convene a meeting at least once in six months. All the adults who are in the voters list of the village are members of the gram sabha.

PANCHAYAT ELECTIONS, 1993

On the eve of the expiry of the term of panchayats in 1992, several writ petitions were filed in the High Court of Karnataka to direct the government to hold elections. A division bench of the High Court directed the state government to hold elections. The government preferred an appeal to the Supreme Court which upheld the direction of the High Court. However, the state government postponed elections several times on one pretext or other.

The state election commissioner was appointed in May 1993 and elections to all the three tiers were declared. Elections to the gram panchayats were fixed for 29 December 1993, and taluk panchayats and zilla panchayats for 23 January 1994. But only the elections to the gram panchayats were conducted as scheduled and others were postponed indefinitely. Out of a total electorate of 2,06,36,782, there were 1,01,93,188 women. Karnataka was the first state to bring its panchayati raj legislation in line with the Constitution (Seventy-third Amendment Act) and to hold elections to the gram panchayats under the new Act.

It may be noted here that as soon as the Janata Dal government came to power in December 1994 it appointed a committee to review the 1993 Act and suggest measures to make panchayats 'institutions of self government' in the true sense of the term.*

The panchayat elections in the state were completed in two phases – 1993 and 1995. The 1993 gram panchayat elections were held under the 1993 Act as passed by the Assembly. The 1995 elections to the other two tiers (taluk and zilla panchayats) were also held under the 1993 Act but just with one amendment relating to the Backward Classes reservations. The amendment introduced two categories of Backward Classes – 'A' and 'B'. 'A' category was considered most backward and 'B' category more backward. The former was given reservation to the extent of 26.6 per cent and the latter 6.4 per cent. Under category 'A' 190 castes were listed and nine castes under category B.

GRAM PANCHAYAT ELECTIONS, 1993

At the gram panchayat level, the elections were fought on a non-party basis. However, the gram panchayat election was an experience in itself. When the panchayat elections were held in Karnataka in December 1993, there were no takers for the 1,239 seats mostly reserved for the Backward Classes, SCs and STs and women. According to the state election authorities, 277 seats were vacant in Mysore district, 253 in Bijapur, 195 in Uttar Kannada, 140 in Belgaum and 109 in Shimoga. The state recorded many strange incidents. In Kalloli gram panchayat seats were auctioned for the welfare of the village. The Janata Dal had proposed about 12 amendments to the Act and threatened to boycott the election if they were not incorporated. Writ petitions questioning the constitutional validity of provisions of the Constitution (Seventy-third Amendment) Act providing reservation for various categories were filed in various High Courts in the country including Karnataka.

---

* The committee submitted its report on 19 March, 1996. Mr. K. S. Krishnaswamy was its first chairman. When he relinquished the office Mr. P. R. Nayak became the chairman.

The election to the offices of the adhyaksha and upadhyaksha was conducted in the first meeting of the gram panchayats. Stray incidents of clashes, kidnapping of members, and forced withdrawal of nominations, including those of women, were reported. The then government gave this as an excuse to postpone the elections to taluk panchayats and zilla panchayats.

Out of 80,631 gram panchayat members who got elected in this election, 35,160 (43.6 per cent) were women. Out of a total of 5,640 gram panchayats, 1,878 (33 per cent) are today headed by women presidents and vice-presidents. An important outcome of the election process was that, although the Act provides for not less than 33 per cent reservation to women, their actual representation came to 43.6 per cent in the gram panchayats.

TALUK AND ZILLA PANCHAYAT ELECTIONS, 1995

There are 175 taluk panchayats (TPs) and 20 zilla panchayats (ZPs) in Karnataka, comprising 3,340 TP members and 919 ZP members. A total of 1,343 (40 per cent) TP seats and 335 (36 per cent) ZP seats were contested by women. The long-awaited elections to the taluk and zilla panchayats were held in three phases on 13, 15 and 18 March 1995, respectively.

Elections were held in three phases for 914 zilla panchayat and 3,300 taluk panchayat seats spread over 20 districts. Five candidates were declared elected unopposed for the zilla panchayats. The number of unopposed members in the taluk panchayats was 40.

Over 2.16 crore voters, including 1.06 crore women, were eligible to exercise their franchise in these elections. A staggering 3,612 candidates were in the fray for 914 zilla panchayat seats, and 11,497 for the 3,300 taluk panchayat seats.

Elaborate security arrangements were made for the different phases of the elections. Adequate police force was deployed at the polling booths. The superintendents of police were expected to personally supervise the security arrangements. Polling officers were given intensive training. The district administration banned holding of public functions or carnivals from 13 to 18 March 1995 in view of the elections. Thus, the state government was determined to hold free and peaceful elections in the districts and taluks.

This was an election with another difference. Unlike in the past, publicity was missing. Vigorous door-to-door campaigning took its place. However, the major political parties launched the campaign using a large number of vehicles splashed with election graffiti.

Repolling was ordered in some zilla panchayat and taluk panchayat constituencies as ballot boxes were allegedly seized from the polling booths. Clashes between supporters of political parties also marred the elections in a few places. Minor skirmishes and suspension of election for a few hours were also reported. Yet these elections were by and large peaceful, and 65 to 72 per cent polling was recorded.

The ruling Janata Dal established its supremacy in the panchayat elections by capturing 19 of the 20 zilla panchayats with a thumping majority. It bagged the post of president in all but the Dakshina Kannada district. Here Janata Dal had to be content with the post of vice-president and had to concede the office of president to Congress (I) because no Janata Dal member belonging to the reserved category was elected in that zilla panchayat. No single party got a majority in Dakshina Kannada zilla panchayat.

PRESENT STUDY

The Institute of Social Sciences took up the present study as a follow-up of its earlier studies on panchayati raj institutions. It aimed to analyse and understand the leadership structure that has emerged as a result of the recent panchayat elections. Another major area of enquiry was the election issues and the election process.

REFERENCES

Abdul Aziz, *History of Panchayat Reforms in Karnataka*, (Mimeo).

Anand Inbanathan, *The New Panchayati Raj System in Karnataka: An Evaluation*, Institute of Social Sciences Manuscript Report Series, New Delhi, 1992.

———, *Karnataka Panchayats under Administrators*, Institute of Social Sciences Occasional Paper Series - 14, New Delhi, 1994.

Bhargava B S and Subha K, 'Political Empowerment of Women. The Case of Karnatakas' Experience with Panchayati Raj', *Political Economy Journal of India*, nos. 3 & 4, July-Dec. 1994.

George Mathew, ed., *Panchayati Raj in Karnataka Today: Its National Dimensions*, Concept Publishing Company, New Delhi, 1986.

———, "Karnataka Puts the Clock Back," *The Hindu*, April 9, 1993.

———, "Karnataka's Political Tragedy," *The Hindu*, May 17, 1994.

T. R. Satish Chandran, 'Karnataka,' in *Status of Panchayati Raj in the States of India 1994*, Concept Publishing Co., New Delhi, 1994.

Part I

PANCHAYAT ELECTIONS

Chapter II

Election Process and Issues

Elections constitute a major political activity for people in a democratic society – they are one of their most important political rights. Elections ensure that the opinions of the citizens are recognised and given due weightage. Grassroots level democracy in local governments is the basic foundation on which the entire democratic edifice rests. Therefore, elections to panchayats in rural areas, where 74 per cent of India's population resides, (in Karnataka the rural population is 69 per cent) assume great significance.

Since Karnataka was one of the first states to complete the panchayat elections to the three tiers, albeit in two phases with an intervening gap of one year, this study probes into the electoral process and the people's participation in these elections. It also focusses on several other issues which affected the elections. The areas of enquiry were:

1. Emergence of new forces at the grassroots level.
2. Participation of women.
3. Participation of Backward Classes.
4. Impact of the 33 per cent reservation for Backward Classes and women.
5. Violence.
6. Propaganda methods.
7. Influence of money, caste and family.
8. Role of political parties.
9. Influence of media.
10. Performance/failure of previous panchayat members.

The study was based on primary and secondary data. It depended largely on interviews which were based on pre-tested questionnaires. Twenty full-time field investigators collected the primary data over a period of two months.

Altogether 3,343 people comprising 3,086 men and 257 women were interviewed to elicit the views regarding various matters related to panchayats and the elections. The respondents were selected from all four divisions as shown in Table 2.1. Secondary data were collected from published reports and articles as well as journals and newspapers.

TABLE 2.1
Areas Selected for Study

Division	No. of Taluks	No. of Gram Panchayats
Bangalore	39	127
Mysore	37	139
Belgaum	56	160
Gulbarga	43	154

Respondents' Profile

About 54.1 per cent of the respondents are below 40 years of age and 25 per cent between 40 and 50 years of age. Vokkaligas and Lingayats constitute the largest caste groups, followed by Brahmins. A majority of the respondents are literate. Illiterates constitute only 3.4 per cent of the sample. Among literates, a large section had studied upto SSLC. The share of graduates is only 15.8 per cent. Respondents include a cross-section of occupational groups like journalists, businessmen, agriculturists, ex-MLA/MP, ex-mandal members, etc. There are also professionals like lawyers, engineers and doctors. The profile of the respondents in terms of their occupation, sex, educational level, caste and religion, and age is shown below in Tables 2.2 to 2.6.

TABLE 2.2
Occupation of Respondents

Occupational Group	No. of Respondents	Percentage
Journalist	126	3.8
Advocate	167	5.0
Doctor	61	1.8
Police/SI	69	2.1
Ex-Mandal member	377	11.3
GP/TB-municipal council member	28	.8
Ex-Zilla parishad member	11	.3
Ex-MLA/MP	12	.4
Mahila/Yuvathi mandal	140	4.2
Yuvaka mandal	256	7.7
Businessman	459	13.7
Agriculturist	348	10.4
Village head/leader	148	4.4
School teacher/Lecturer	460	13.8
NGO staff	33	1.0
Others	648	19.4
Total	3,343	100.0

TABLE 2.3
Gender of Respondents

Gender	No. of Respondents	Percentage
Men	3,086	92.3
Women	257	7.7
Total	3,343	100.0

TABLE 2.4
Educational Level of Respondents

Educational Level	No. of Respondents	Percentage
Illiterate	114	3.4
Literate	14	.4
Lower primary	157	4.7
Higher primary	418	12.5
Secondary (8th to 10th std.)	207	6.2
SSLC	732	21.9
PUC	354	10.6
Degree	529	15.8
Postgraduation	164	4.9
Law	201	6.0
Engineering	28	.8
Diploma	34	1.0
Medicine	59	1.8
B.Ed/M.Ed	137	4.1
Teacher higher course (TCH)	165	4.9
Any other	30	.9
Total	3,343	100.0

TABLE 2.5
Caste and Religion of Respondents

Caste	No. of Respondents	Percentage
Adi Karnataka (AK)	132	3.9
Adi Dravidian (AD)	6	.2
Bhovi	16	.5
Gowda/Vokkaliga	574	17.2
Lingayat	919	27.5
Brahmin	318	9.5
Bunt/Rai/Shetty	53	1.6
Kodava	17	.5
Konkani Nayak	6	.2
Naidu	1	.0
Reddy	55	1.6
Madiwalar	11	.3
Banajiga (Setty)	30	.9
Kuruba	174	5.2
Lambani	29	.9
Gonda	4	.1
Maratha	58	1.7
Naik	86	2.6
Christian	28	.8
Muslim	143	4.3
Other Hindus	683	20.4
Total	3,343	100.0

TABLE 2.6
Age Distribution of Respondents

Age Group	No. of Respondents	Percentage
Upto 25 years	224	6.7
26 to 30 years	520	15.6
31 to 35 years	480	14.4
36 to 40 years	582	17.4
41 to 50 years	830	24.8
51 to 60 years	519	15.5
61 to 70 years	138	4.1
71 years & above	50	1.5
Total	3,343	100.0

Information about the Election

Information can be of great importance in educating and influencing the common man. Table 2.7 shows the sources of information at the local level.

Most of the respondents were aware of the panchayat elections. As Table 2.7 shows, their first source of information was newspapers. Almost an equal percentage (i.e., 79 per cent) gathered information from radio and television. Thus we see that the reach of the print and electronic media in the villages is expanding. A considerable percentage of people (i.e., 29.76 per cent) learnt about elections from political parties and only a small percentage mentioned other sources like friends, neighbours, market place etc.

TABLE 2.7
Source of Information about the Election

Source of Information	No. of Respondents	Percentage
Newspapers	2,837	84.87
Radio/TV	2641	79.00
Political party	995	29.76
NGO	38	1.14
Market place	203	6.10
People	908	27.16

Note: The percentage increases due multiple response.

Campaign Methods

Political communication becomes crucial at the time of elections. A campaign is the most important way to shape opinions. The contestants come into direct contact with their voters in many ways as shown in Table 2.8.

TABLE 2.8
Methods of Campaign

Campaigning Methods	No. of Respondents	Percentage
Door to door/Home visit	2,916	87.22
Handbills	1,508	45.11
Wall writings	228	6.82
Loudspeakers	880	26.32
Posters	331	9.90
Public meetings	508	15.20
Newspapers	92	2.75
Video/Audio	4	0.12
Others	194	5.80

Note: The percentage increases due to multiple response.

Visiting personally by going to each house is the main method of campaign as reported by 87.22 per cent of the respondents. Handbills and loudspeakers are the other two channels that are popular. Only 15.20 per cent reported public meetings and 9.90 per cent wall posters and wall writings. People also pointed out newspapers' campaigning on elections.

Role of Non-Governmental Organisations (NGOs)

NGOs have a major role in awakening the masses and mobilising them. They can act as powerful agencies of social and political change by influencing the thinking of the people. During panchayat elections their role can become particularly important as they have the strongest links with people.

TABLE 2.9
Presence of NGOs

Presence	No. of Respondents	Percentage
Yes	720	21.5
No	2,623	78.5
Total	3,343	100.0

TABLE 2.10
Role of NGOs

Role	No. of Respondents	Percentage
Not playing any role	3,084	92.3
Put up the candidate	50	1.5
Support the party	86	2.6
Held separate campaign	66	2.0
Conducted workshops	57	1.7
Total	3,343	100.0

However, in the present study, it was found that most of respondents, i.e., 78.5 per cent were not aware of the presence of NGOs. In tune with this observation, it was also found that 92.3 per cent of respondents denied any special role played by NGOs. As evident from Table 2.10, NGOs hardly put up their candidates or conduct awareness camps or workshops to influence the election process.

Fairness of Elections

A recurrent feature of our elections is the irregularities and frauds which occur frequently. In order to understand the nature of the recent elections, respondents were asked to give their opinion on this issue. They are as shown in Tables 2.11 and 2.12.

TABLE 2.11
Elections Fair or Not Fair

Fairness of Election	No. of Respondents	Percentage
Completely fair	2,724	81.5
Some problems	489	14.6
Not fair	86	2.6
Do not know	44	1.3
Total	3,343	100.0

TABLE 2.12
Reasons for Unfair Elections

Reasons	No. of Respondents	Percentage
No information	2,813	84.1
Rigging	195	5.8
Booth capturing	26	.8
Kidnapping	28	.8
Others	281	8.4
Total	3,343	100.0

Caste Affinity

The rural power structure has been usually associated with caste. It has been observed that caste plays an important role and that voters tend to elect representatives belonging to their own caste and community. Responses to the role of this factor in the election process are shown in Table 2.13.

TABLE 2.13
Caste Affinity

Caste Affinity	No. of Respondents	Percentage
Yes	1,195	35.7
No	2,113	63.2
Do not know	35	1.0
Total	3,343	100.0

It is worth noting that the role of caste as a powerful factor influencing elections is reducing. Only 35.7 per cent said that caste influenced the election while 63.2 per cent reported that it did not have any influence on the election process.

TABLE 2.14
Directions given by Caste/Religious Leaders

Directions given	No. of Respondents	Percentage
Yes	514	15.4
No	2,737	81.9
Do not know	92	2.8
Total	3,343	100.0

Religious leaders and heads of caste groups also did not play any significant role. Almost 82 per cent denied observing such leaders giving any directions regarding the selection of the candidates (Table 2.14).

Influence of Money Power

Elections are influenced by many factors. It is widely believed that money power is one such important factor. The responses to the role of money in elections are given in Table 2.15. Fifty-four per cent of the respondents say that money has influenced elections.

TABLE 2.15
Influence of Money on Elections

Influencing Factors	No. of Respondents	Percentage
Yes	1,815	54.3
No	1,381	41.3
Do not know	147	4.4
Total	3,343	100.0

TABLE 2.15a
Influence of Various Material Inducements on Elections

Influencing Factors	No. of Respondents	Percentage
Money: to some extent	902	27.00
Money: to great extent	315	9.40
Alcohol	1,954	58.45
Foodgrains/Clothes, etc	270	8.10
Dinner	669	20.00
Others	160	4.79

Apart from money, other material inducements were also offered (Table 2.15a). The supply of alcohol and providing dinner are considered to be the other two most influential factors in the elections. Twenty per cent said that sumptuous meals were offered to the villagers. Almost 59 per cent said alcohol was distributed. Even here there was discrimination – beer and foreign liquor were given to the well-off, and local *arrack* to the poor.

Voters' Preference

It is noteworthy to point out here that individual qualities and achievements have greater influence than the party, caste and education of the candidates in elections. Table 2.16 shows that 46.55 per cent of the people voted for a particular candidate because they considered him/her to be a good person. Only 11.48 per cent voted keeping in mind party affiliation. Efficiency and previous performance were also given weightage. The former is considered very essential – 22.30 per cent voted for efficient candidates.

TABLE 2.16
Reasons for Voting for Particular Candidate

Reasons	No. of Respondents	Percentage
Not voted	268	7.66
Good person	1,556	46.55
Interested in social work	246	7.36
Own party candidate	384	11.48
Own caste/relative	46	1.37
Own village	64	1.90
Previous performance	71	2.12
Educated	35	1.10
Efficient	747	22.30
Others	96	2.90

Major Issues in the Election

Failure of the previous representatives to deliver the goods was a major issue for a sizeable section of the people. Split in the then ruling party and the coming to power of the Janata Dal was another. Respondents also considered corruption and poverty to be important issues. It appears that issues of national importance like Babri Masjid, Hindutva, etc., have not played a major role (Table 2.17).

TABLE 2.17
Issues in the Election

Issues	No. of Respondents	Percentage
Dalit	283	8.46
Women	348	10.40
Failure of previous members	1,518	45.40
Corruption	1,118	33.44
Babri Masjid	1,59	4.75
Poverty	685	20.50
Split in party	1,310	39.20
Hindutva	185	5.50
Others	753	22.50

Violence

Violence is commonly observed during elections. In order to find out whether violence is a part of local level elections, respondents were asked a specific question on the issue. A huge majority, 92.6 per cent, did not report violence. However, a small percentage, 6.3 per cent, mentioned violence during elections, as is seen in Table 2.18. Stray incidents of group clashes, stone pelting and murder were mentioned (Table 2.19).

TABLE 2.18
Violence during Elections

Violence during Elections	No. of Respondents	Percentage
Yes	210	6.3
No	3,095	92.6
Do not know	38	1.1
Total	3,343	100.0

TABLE 2.19
Type of Violence

Violence	No. of Respondents	Percentage
No information	3,177	95.0
Stone pelting	6	.2
Stabbing	2	.1
Group clash	108	3.2
Murder	1	.0
Others	49	1.5
Total	3,343	100.0

Change in Government

Wherever there is a change in the party in power, there is a simultaneous change in the political life of the people. It was worth probing whether the electorate observed any change in the functioning of the government and whether such a change affected the elections.

Respondents were almost equally divided on the question whether the coming to power of the Janata Dal government had influenced the election. Table 2.20 shows that 49.4 per cent felt that the change of government in the state had affected the panchayat elections.

TABLE 2.20
Change of Government

Any Change	No. of Respondents	Percentage
Yes	1,652	49.4
No	1,629	48.7
Do not know	62	1.9
Total	3,343	100.0

Political ideology appears to have had a great influence. It is interesting to see that 15.1 per cent attributed the impact of the change in government to the ideology of the ruling Janata Dal, 12.6 per cent said that its leadership was trustworthy. The effect of the change of government in the election is shown in Table 2.21.

TABLE 2.21
Aspects of Change as Influencing Factors

Reasons	No. of Respondents	Percentage
No information	1,754	52.5
Political ideology	367	11.0
Trust in leadership	421	12.6
Leadership qualities	119	3.6
Previous record	178	5.3
Ruling political party	504	15.1
Total	3,343	100.0

Difference between 1993 and 1995 Elections

Regarding the differences between the 1993 gram panchayat and the 1995 elections to the other two tiers, opinion is equally divided between those who see some difference and those who do not (Tables 2.22 and 2.22a).

TABLE 2.22
Difference between 1993 and 1995 Elections

Difference	No. of Respondents	Percentage
Yes	1,540	46.1
No	1,572	47.0
Do not know	231	6.9
Total	3,343	100.0

It is clear from Table 2.22a that most of the respondents could clearly differentiate between the partyless elections to the gram panchayats and party-based elections to the other two tiers. The 1993 election appears to have been expensive as reported by 4.78 per cent; the 1995 election was found to be inexpensive by 7.18 per cent of the respondents. During the 1995 elections Seshan's influence was obvious (8.62 per cent).

The 1995 panchayat elections was held immediately after the November 1994 assembly elections. The assembly election was generally considered a 'sober' one without extravagant expenditure and too much noise. This positive trend was attributed to the stringent election code implemented by the Central Election Commission. T. N. Seshan, the Chief Election Commissioner, was credited with this achievement and popularly considered as 'Seshan effect.' The State Election Commission which conducted the panchayat elections about four months after the assembly elections could effectively continue the assembly election ethos. 8.62 per cent respondents stated that 'Seshan effect' was clearly evident in the panchayat election too.

TABLE 2.22a
Difference between 1993 and 1995 Elections

Difference	No. of Respondents	Percentage
1993		
Partyless elections	677	20.25
Influence of local issues	3	0.09
Caste politics	17	0.51
Not expensive	91	2.72
Violence	39	1.17
Expensive	160	4.78
1995		
Party based elections	661	19.77
Sheshan's influence	288	8.62
Violence	6	0.18
Expensive election	88	2.63
Not expensive	240	7.18
Others	253	7.57

Reservation Policy

The system of reservation of seats in the PRIs was introduced to mobilise the hitherto politically unorganised members, namely women and other weaker sections of the society. It would be of interest to see whether people accept this policy and how they perceive it. Respondents were asked to express their feelings about the issue. The responses are shown in Tables 2.23 to 2.24a.

A huge 80 per cent welcomed the reservation of one-third of the seats for women, showing its widespread acceptance. The main reason cited was that it ensures equality. However, 19.4 per cent are of the opinion that reservation should be on the basis of education. Out of 3,343 respondents, 201 who are against reservation for women because they feel that women are illiterate and incapable of participating in panchayati raj institutions (Table 2.23a).

TABLE 2.23
Attitude towards 33 Per Cent Reservation for Women

Reservation for Women	No. of Respondents	Percentage
Yes	2,683	80.3
No	650	19.4
No information	10	.3
Total	3,343	100.0

TABLE 2.23a
Reasons for Welcoming or Opposing Reservation for Women

Reasons	No. of Respondents	Percentage
No information	1,117	33.4
Should be on education	467	14.0
Equality	939	28.1
50% should be given	85	2.5
Corruption may be reduced	99	3.0
Panchayats' function affected	174	5.2
Should be reduced	78	2.3
Women cannot function effectively	102	3.1
No time to spend in panchayat	7	.2
Illiterate/Not capable	201	6.0
Others	74	2.2
Total	3,343	100.0

TABLE 2.24
Attitude towards 33 Per Cent Reservation for Other Backward Classes (OBC)

Reservation for OBC	No. of Respondents	Percentage
Yes	2,432	72.7
No	883	26.4
No information/Do not know	28	.8
Total	3,343	100.0

TABLE 2.24a

Reasons for Welcoming or Opposing Reservation for Other Backward Classes (OBC)

Reasons	No. of Respondents	Percentage
No response	1,901	56.8
Should be based on education	242	7.2
Social justice	931	27.8
It should be reduced	87	2.6
Equal opportunity	88	2.6
Opposing the reservation	58	1.7
Others	36	1.1
Total	3,343	100.0

TABLE 2.25

Opinion about Panchayats under Administrators

Opinions	No. of Respondents	Percentage
No response	2,520	75.4
Progress in development	76	2.3
Steady development	16	.5
High corruption	143	4.3
Acted like dictators	10	.3
People have no access	105	3.1
Careless attitude	120	3.6
No partiality	105	3.1
Others	248	7.4
Total	3,343	100.0

When asked the reasons for supporting this measure, 28.1 per cent of respondents believed that it would establish gender equality. Three per cent of the respondents expected women representatives to be less corrupt. Only 2.5 per cent supported 50 per cent reservation for women. Some of the respondents did not show faith in women's leadership. Six per cent felt that women are illiterate and incapable. Another 3.1 per cent felt that women cannot function effectively as people,s representatives.

One-third reservation for Other Backward Classes is welcomed by 72.7 per cent of the respondents, while 26.4 per cent are against it (Table 2.24). While 56.8 per cent cannot give any reason why they support or oppose it, 27.8 per cent feel that it ensures social justice and 2.6 per cent equal opportunity. (Table 2.24a).

About 28 per cent felt that it is only through reservation that the underprivileged can be involved in decision-making and social justice be achieved. This measure gives scope for wider representation and for improving the quality of participation. About 7.2 per cent felt that the members should be selected on the basis of their education.

Panchayats under Administrators

The bureaucracy provides stability between elections. On expiry of the term of local bodies, administrators are appointed till the next elections. In the recent past the rural local bodies were dissolved and placed under administrative rule for a short period. The respondents were asked queries in this regard.

The respondents were not in a position to express clearly their opinion about the period under administrators. About 75 per cent of the respondents had no opinion. About 11 per cent reported that it was a phase of poor administration (Table 2.25). High corruption in the absence of an elected body was reported by 4.3 per cent. Careless attitude of the administrators and lack of accessibility were also mentioned. Only 3.1 per cent said the administrators ruled without any partiality.

Chapter III

Democracy at Work

The legitimacy of elections as crucial instruments of a democratic political process cannot be denied at the local level. Elections determine the fate of rulers. The present study focussed on the main issues which affected the panchayat elections and the election process itself. A summary of the findings along with our reflections are given in this chapter.

The study brings out certain trends regarding the sources of political information in rural areas in Karnataka. Most of the people mentioned newspapers, radio and television as the media through which they came to know of the elections. Our data confirm that traditional sources like the market place and neighbourhood are receding into the background. The electorate though open to various kinds of issues and ideologies, examined and evaluated the previous performance of the candidates. Non-performance of the members of the 1987-92 panchayats was the main issue which decided the voting pattern. Most of them voted for a candidate because the contestant was a good person and was socially active.

Almost half of the respondents observed that alcohol was distributed during the elections. Clothes and foodgrains were the other material inducements offered to influence the voters. Sumptuous meals were provided to villagers. The rich and influential were treated to beer and foreign liquor, while the poor were given *arrack* and such other locally made spirits. However, the respondents were almost equally divided on the issue of influence of money in the elections. Regarding the election campaign, door-to-door visits were mentioned as the most popular method, followed by distribution of handbills. Other forms like public meetings, wall posters, use of loudspeakers were secondary.

Reservation is supported as the first step in bringing about gender equality. People also welcome reservation for OBCs. These measures are expected to enable wider representation and prevent dominance of the traditional elite.

The change over to Janata Dal government and the political ideology of the new government influenced the elections. Respondents also said that the leadership was trustworthy. The past performance of candidates, the organisational politics of political parties, and their ideologies were significant concerns in the elections. Corruption was also mentioned as having decided the outcome. Issues like Hindutva and Babri Masjid did not appear to be of great significance at the local level.

An interesting finding is that most of the respondents reported absence of violence during elections. Even those who mentioned it found to be of a low degree.

The study revealed that there is a trend towards a multiparty system, and that party ideology is of significance. Caste is losing its importance as a major factor, and individual achievements are becoming decisive.

The existence of more than one political party implies competition. The role of political parties is becoming progressively more important in panchayati raj elections (see Table 3.1 and 3.2). They have come to play a major role in recruiting candidates to panchayat positions. Therefore, they must take up the responsibility of training potential leaders. The parties can form a training wing along with a women's wing to develop in their members the skills of running PRIs effectively. They should also take up the responsibility of creating awareness about the programmes under the panchayats and devising pre- and post-training activities.

It is a commendable achievement on the part of the Janata Dal government to have conducted the hitherto oft-postponed elections so promptly and in a free and peaceful manner. Violence was sporadic in this election; it was by and large peaceful, free and frank. Caste has began to play a lesser role in

TABLE 3.1

Seats Won by Political Parties in the 1995 Elections
Taluk Panchayats in Karnataka

Sl. No.	Name of the Districts	No. of TP Seats	BJP	Cong (I)	CPI	CPI (M)	Ind.	JD	KCP
1.	Bangalore (U)	69 (27)	12	19	-	-	1	37	-
2.	Bangalore (R)	143 (57)	11	15	-	-	2	115	-
3.	Chitradurga	172 (70)	18	56	-	-	11	81	6
4.	Kolar	186 (80)	-	69	-	3	2	112	-
5.	Shimoga	148 (62)	26	38	-	-	11	59	14
6.	Tumkur	203 (80)	15	66	-	-	15	102	5
7.	Chickmagalur	105 (46)	2	17	2	-	7	77	-
8.	D. Kannada	206 (82)	79	60	-	1	2	61	3
9.	Hassan	143 (56)	2	15	-	-	4	122	-
10.	Kodagu	48 (19)	18	4	-	-	-	26	-
11.	Mandya	147 (56)	3	40	-	-	19	85	-
12.	Mysore	243 (94)	7	77	-	-	27	129	3
13.	Belgaum	287 (107)	-	68	-	-	46	172	1
14.	Bijapur	226 (84)	10	57	-	-	5	154	-
15.	Dharwad	248 (106)	9	63	-	-	10	166	-
16.	U. Kannada	123 (57)	10	9	-	-	-	104	-
17.	Bellary	137 (55)	1	48	-	-	4	82	2
18.	Bidar	107 (43)	12	32	-	-	6	57	-
19.	Gulbarga	204 (81)	4	59	-	4	6	101	30
20.	Raichur	195 (81)	1	75	-	1	9	109	-
	TOTAL	3,340 (1343)	240	887	2	9	187	1951	64

Note: Figures in brackets indicate seats reserved for women.
Source: Karnataka Election Commission.

TABLE 3.2

Seats Won by Political Parties in the 1995 Elections Zilla Panchayats in Karnataka

Sl. No.	Name of the Districts	No. of ZP Seats	BJP	Cong (I)	CPI	CPI (M)	IND	JD	KRRS	KCP
1.	Bangalore (U)	18 (7)	2	4	-	-	-	12	-	-
2.	Bangalore (R)	38 (15)	4	1	-	-	-	33	-	-
3.	Chitradurga	46 (17)	6	14	-	-	2	24	-	-
4.	Kolar	50 (19)	-	14	-	1	-	35	-	-
5.	Shimoga	41 (15)	7	10	-	-	-	18	1	5
6.	Tumkur	54 (20)	4	16	-	-	5	29	-	-
7.	Chickmagalur	33 (13)	-	3	-	-	2	28	-	-
8.	D. Kannada	55 (19)	25	14	-	1	-	15	-	-
9.	Hassan	37 (13)	-	3	-	-	1	33	-	-
10.	Kodagu	27 (10)	7	5	-	-	-	15	-	-
11.	Mandya	39 (14)	-	7	-	-	-	30	2	-
12.	Mysore	64 (22)	2	19	-	-	3	40	-	-
13.	Belgaum	76 (27)	-	10	-	-	12	54	-	-
14.	Bijapur	60 (22)	-	9	-	-	-	51	-	-
15.	Dharwad	67 (24)	-	15	-	-	-	52	-	-
16.	U. Kannada	38 (14)	2	-	-	-	-	36	-	-
17.	Bellary	38 (15)	-	10	-	-	1	27	-	-
18.	Bidar	29 (11)	2	5	-	-	-	22	-	-
19.	Gulbarga	55 (19)	2	16	-	1	-	27	-	9
20.	Raichur	54 (19)	-	17	-	-	2	34	1	-
	TOTAL	919 (335)	63	192	-	3	28	615	4	14

Note: Figures in brackets indicate seats reserved for women.
Source: Karnataka Election Commission.

the grassroots democratic process because of state intervention. People appreciate the entrance of new political forces like women and members belonging to the deprived sections in a big way.

Respondents feel that educated women should contest the local elections. Thus political and social education is the need of the hour. As noted earlier, this responsibility should be shared by political parties, the government, and voluntary organisations. Attention should be focussed on the human resource development aspect.

It is said information is power and information should be shared with the common man. Now that the electronic media has reached most villages, serious thought should be given to developing satellite, radio and TV programmes on panchayati raj political issues.

The electorate no longer ignores the performance of the local political leaders, which implies that the work of the representatives during their tenure is of great significance. Only when they spend their time resolving the problems of their constituencies, can they rely on the support of the voters.

It must be emphasised that the electorate cannot be taken for granted; their role in maintaining and preserving a democratic regime should not be underestimated. There is a high degree of issue-orientation and political understanding among them. Voters have become highly politicised; they vote in their own interest.

Though the bureaucracy provides stable leadership when the elected body is in a state of flux, the respondents have preferred elected bodies. They are optimistic about the prospects of the democratic process, though there was little indication that they had carefully analysed the period of administrative rule. They are sceptical about the administrators and critical of their inaccessibility.

However, administrators have a decisive role in translating

various policies and programmes of the government into reality. The efficacy of decentralised planning depends on their commitment. They must, therefore, be oriented towards the local self-governing bodies. This presupposes a drastic and purposive change in their outlook. Placed in positions of authority and responsibility, they can reactivate the political process and create a better climate.

The administrative process therefore needs to be reformed. This demands trained personnel with the requisite skills and a commitment to developmental goals.

The election procedure seems to be reasonably efficient but a close examination has revealed some weaknesses. Still, the study found graphic demonstrations of people's belief in their capacity to govern themselves. Effective methods of election administration have a direct impact on the accuracy and honesty of elections. A start has been made by giving due attention to the election machinery and the election process. The reforming zeal of the government in power can further strengthen this in the interest of honesty and efficiency.

Part II

SOCIAL BACKGROUND OF ELECTED REPRESENTATIVES

Chapter IV

Emerging Leadership

This chapter looks at the socio-economic backgrounds, political profile and motivational forces of the emerging leadership. Altogether 4,775 elected panchayat members were interviewed (out of this 1,931 were women) using a pre-tested questionnaire. They were from all levels of the panchayati raj institutions. The results are presented in a tabular form.

SOCIAL PROFILE OF THE PANCHAYAT MEMBERS

Age Distribution

Overall, the data (Table 4.1) show that more than 60 per cent of them are less than 40 years of age. The share of this group is higher at the taluk panchayat than at the gram panchayat and zilla panchayat levels. This indicates that the younger generation is showing more interest in panchayati raj institutions.

Marital Status

Traditionally, marriage is the norm in Indian society, especially in rural India. Table 4.2 gives the marital status of elected members.

The data show that more than 90 per cent of the members are married. However, their percentage is marginally less in the case of gram panchayats. The share of single persons is higher at the taluk panchayat level. This may be due to the fact that at this level nearly 50 per cent of the members are below 35 years of age. There is a representation of devadasis at the gram panchayat level—16 out of 4,017 elected members.

TEBLE 4.1

Age Distribution of Panchayat Members

Age Group	GP	TP	ZP	Overall
Upto 25 years	82 (5.5)	139 (12.3)	21 (4.1)	272 (5.7)
26 to 30 years	643 (16.0)	39 (16.0)	66 (12.8)	748 (15.7)
31 to 35 years	800 (19.9)	50 (20.6)	99 (19.2)	949 (19.9)
36 to 40 years	854 (21.3)	53 (21.8)	114 (22.1)	1,021 (21.4)
41 to 50 years	1,025 (25.5)	52 (21.4)	157 (30.5)	1,234 (25.8)
51 to 60 years	356 (8.9)	17 (7.0)	50 (9.7)	423 (8.9)
61 to 70 years	99 (2.5)	1 (0.4)	5 (1.0)	105 (2.2)
71 years & above	19 (0.5)	1 (0.4)	3 (0.6)	23 (0.5)
Total	4,017 (100)	243 (100)	515 (100)	4,775 (100)

Notes: (1) GP - Gram Panchayat TP - Taluk Panchayat ZP - Zilla Panchayat.
(2) Figures in brackets are percentages.

TABLE 4.2
Marital Status of Panchayat Members

Marital Status	GP	TP	ZP	Overall
Married	3,602 (89.7)	224 (92.2)	486 (94.4)	4,312 (90.3)
Single	228 (5.7)	15 (6.2)	23 (4.5)	266 (5.6)
Widow/Widower	163 (4.1)	4 (1.6)	6 (1.2)	173 (3.6)
Divorced	8 (0.2)	0 (0.0)	0 (0.0)	8 (0.2)
Devadasi	16 (0.4)	0 (0.0)	0 (0.0)	16 (0.3)
Total	4,017 (100.00)	243 (100.00)	515 (100.00)	4,775 (100.00)

Note: Figures in brackets are percentages.

Family Size

Data on family size and the number of children of the members are important for understanding whether the joint family system is still intact in the villages and whether the elected members practise family planning.

From Table 4.3 it can be observed that the average size of the family is 5 to 10 at all levels. Sixty-seven per cent of the members have a family size in this range. A look at the number of children in the family will indicate whether the large size of the family is due to the joint family system or the large number of children in individual families.

An analysis of the number of children (Table 4.3a) shows that only in 20 per cent of the households there are two children. About 44 per cent of the elected members have three to four children. The percentage of members with three to four children is highest at the zilla panchayat level. At the gram panchayat and taluk panchayat levels 13 per cent of the members have five to six children. Thus a medium-sized family is still the norm in rural areas.

TABLE 4.3

Family Size of the Panchayat Members

Total Family Members	GP	TP	ZP	Overall
Upto 4	736 (18.3)	39 (16.0)	76 (14.8)	851 (17.8)
5 to 10	2,725 (67.8)	155 (63.8)	353 (68.5)	3,233 (67.7)
11 to 15	347 (8.6)	31 (12.8)	59 (11.5)	437 (9.2)
16 to 20	125 (3.1)	9 (3.7)	16 (3.1)	150 (3.1)
21 to 30	58 (1.4)	5 (2.1)	5 (1.0)	68 (1.4)
31 to 40	19 (0.5)	3 (1.2)	3 (0.6)	25 (0.5)
41 to 60	5 (0.1)	1 (0.4)	3 (0.6)	9 (0.2)
61 & above	2 (0.0)	-	-	2 (0.0)
Total	4,017 (100)	243 (100)	515 (100)	4,775 (100)

Note: Figures in brackets are percentages.

TABLE 4.3a

Number of Children of Panchayat Members

No. of Children	GP	TP	ZP	Overall
No children	400 (10.0)	23 (9.5)	45 (8.7)	468 (9.8)
Only one	330 (8.2)	24 (9.9)	40 (7.8)	394 (8.3)
Only two	803 (20.0)	56 (23.0)	112 (21.7)	971 (20.3)
3 to 4	1,737 (43.2)	104 (42.8)	253 (49.1)	2,094 (43.9)
5 to 6	549 (13.7)	31 (12.8)	53 (10.3)	633 (13.3)
7 to 8	143 (3.6)	5 (2.1)	8 (1.6)	156 (3.3)
9 to 10	44 (1.1)	-	4 (0.8)	48 (1.0)
11 & above	11 (0.3)	-	-	11 (0.2)
Total	4,017	243	515	4,775

Note: Figures in brackets are percentages.

Religion

Religion plays an important role at the village level. The distribution of elected members across religious communities was analysed to understand the representation of minorities.

A majority of the elected members are Hindus. There is some representation of Muslims. Their representation is relatively greater at the gram panchayat and taluk panchayat than at the zilla panchayat levels.

TABLE 4.4
Religious Affiliation of Panchayat Members

Religion	GP	TP	ZP	Overall
Hindu	3,795 (94.5)	230 (94.7)	501 (97.3)	4,526 (94.8)
Muslim	197 (4.9)	10 (4.1)	11 (2.1)	218 (4.6)
Christian	19 (0.5)	3 (1.2)	2 (0.4)	24 (0.5)
Others	6 (0.1)	-	1 (0.2)	7 (0.1)
Total	4,017 (100)	243 (100)	515 (100)	4,775 (100)

Note: Figures in brackets are percentages.

Caste

Table 4.5 indicates the parametric trends of the caste composition of the population under study. As per the 1991 census majority of the Indian population come from Backward Caste (BC) communities. Out of 4,775 elected members we interviewed, 1938 belong to BCs which forms 40.5 per cent. Another interesting aspect is that the number of elected representatives who belong to the backward castes shows a gradual increase as we go up from lower tier of the panchayats to the higher. From our survey we find that at the gram panchayat level, the members belonging to the BC communities is 39 per cent as against 44.4 per cent at the taluk panchayat level and nearly 50 per cent at the zilla panchayat level. Two vocal and politically powerful castes in Karnataka – the Vokkaligas and the Lingayats – constituted 14 and 17 per cent respectively among the total elected representatives we studied. At the taluk level, the number of Vokkaligas among the elected representatives is more and at the zilla panchayat level the Lingayats have taken the first place.

TABLE 4.5
Caste Composition of Panchayat Members

Caste	GP	TP	ZP	Overall
Adi Karnataka (SC)	503 (12.5)	23 (9.5)	35 (6.8)	561 (11.7)
Adi Dravida (SC)	80 (2.0)	1 (0.4)	5 (1.0)	86 (1.8)
Bhovi (SC)	76 (1.9)	2 (0.8)	10 (1.9)	88 (1.8)
Gowda/Vokkaliga	543 (13.5)	45 (18.5)	84 (16.3)	672 (14.1)
Lingayat	676 (16.8)	37 (15.2)	100 (19.4)	813 (17.0)
Brahmin	100 (2.5)	8 (3.3)	12 (2.3)	120 (2.5)
Bunt/Rai/Shetty	35 (0.9)	2 (0.8)	8 (1.6)	45 (0.9)
Kodava	14 (0.3)	-	3 (0.6)	17 (0.4)
Reddy	62 (1.5)	5 (2.1)	9 (1.7)	76 (1.6)
Madiwalar	16 (0.4)	1 (0.4)	3 (0.6)	20 (0.4)
Banajiga	29 (0.7)	1 (0.4)	1 (0.2)	31 (0.6)
Kuruba	275 (6.8)	22 (9.1)	60 (11.7)	357 (7.5)

table continued...

TABLE 4.5 *contd.*

Caste	GP	TP	ZP	Overall
Lambani/Soliga (ST)	71 (1.8)	12 (4.9)	16 (3.1)	99 (2.1)
Gonda (ST)	24 (0.6)	-	1 (0.2)	25 (0.5)
Maratha	73 (1.8)	2 (0.8)	11 (2.1)	86 (1.8)
Naik (ST)	177 (4.4)	12 (4.9)	20 (3.9)	209 (4.4)
Others	1,041 (25.1)	57 (23.5)	121 (23.9)	1,216 (25.4)
Muslim/Christian and others	222 (5.5)	13 (5.3)	14 (2.7)	249 (5.2)
Total	4,017 (100)	243 (100)	515 (100)	4,775 (100)

Note: Figures in brackets are percentages.

Overall, ST population at all the three tiers has not exceeded 5 per cent (the ST population of Karnataka is 4.26 per cent). At the taluk panchayat level the ST representation is slightly higher than other tiers. In the 'Others' category, minor castes are included which constitutes 25.4 per cent. The Minority communities are Muslims, Christians, Jains and Sikhs. They constitute 5.2 per cent of the total elected representatives we interviewed (Table 4.5).

Educational Status

Education plays an important role in building opinions and shaping attitudes. An analysis of the educational status of the members is presented in Table 4.6.

The data reveal maximum illiteracy at the gram panchayat level. Compared to 11.2 per cent at the gram panchayat level, 2.1 per cent at the taluk panchayat, and 1.2 per cent at the zilla panchayat levels are illiterate. At the gram panchayat level 15.4 per cent can only read and write; 8.8 per cent are graduates. The share of graduates among the taluk panchayat and gram panchayat members is 12.2 per cent and 29.6 per cent, respectively. Among professionals, lawyers dominate at all levels.

TABLE 4.6

Educational Level of Panchayat Members

Educational Level	GP	TP	ZP	Overall
Illiterate	448 (11.2)	5 (2.1)	6 (1.2)	459 (9.6)
Literate	617 (15.4)	10 (4.1)	11 (2.1)	638 (13.4)
Primary (<=4th Std.)	567 (14.1)	22 (9.1)	20 (3.9)	609 (12.8)
Higher primary (4th - 7th)	784 (19.5)	42 (17.3)	58 (11.3)	884 (18.5)
Secondary (Upto 10th)	407 (10.1)	34 (14.0)	65 (12.6)	506 (10.6)
SSLC	538 (13.4)	48 (19.8)	107 (20.8)	693 (14.5)
Pre-University Course	247 (6.1)	32 (13.2)	72 (14.0)	351 (7.4)
Degree	311 (7.7)	36 (14.8)	123 (23.9)	470 (9.8)

Table 4.6 continued...

TABLE 4.6 *Contd.*

Educational Level	GP	TP	ZP	Overall
Postgraduation	16 (0.4)	5 (2.1)	16 (3.1)	37 (0.8)
Law	23 (0.6)	4 (1.6)	17 (3.3)	44 (0.9)
Engineering	9 (0.2)	1 (0.4)	6 (1.2)	16 (0.3)
Diploma	24 (0.6)	2 (0.8)	8 (1.6)	34 (0.7)
Medicine	6 (0.1)	1 (0.4)	3 (0.6)	10 (0.2)
B Ed/M Ed	8 (0.2)	-	3 (0.6)	11 (0.2)
Any other	12 (0.3)	1 (0.4)	-	13 (0.3)
Total	4,017 (100)	243 (100)	515 (100)	4,775 (100)

Note: Figures in brackets are percentages.

Occupation

The occupational classification of the members shows which groups controls the panchayats. The main occupation of the members is presented in Table 4.7 and the secondary occupations in Table 4.7a.

The data show that cultivation is the main occupation, followed by domestic work. Agricultural labour is another important occupation at the gram panchayat level, while at the taluk panchayat level it is self-employment. Very few members – 7 out of 515 at the zilla panchayats, 4 out of 243 at the taluk panchayat, and 19 out of 4,017 at the gram panchayat level – are working as full-time party workers.

TABLE 4.7
Main Occupation of Panchayat Members

Occupation	GP	TP	ZP	Overall
Cultivation	2,469 (61.5)	143 (58.8)	329 (63.9)	2,941 (61.6)
Craftsmen	43 (1.1)	3 (1.2)	2 (0.4)	48 (1.0)
Self-employment	160 (4.0)	14 (5.8)	13 (2.5)	187 (3.9)
Domestic work	710 (17.7)	52 (21.4)	127 (24.7)	889 (18.6)
Petty trader	139 (3.5)	9 (3.7)	10 (1.9)	158 (3.3)
Cottage industry (Wage labourer)	19 (0.5)	1 (0.4)	1 (0.2)	21 (0.4)
Teacher/Lecturer	5 (0.1)	1 (0.4)	1 (0.2)	7 (0.1)
Contractor	31 (0.8)	4 (1.6)	3 (0.6)	38 (0.8)
Full-time party work	19 (0.5)	4 (1.6)	7 (1.4)	30 (0.6)
Agricultural labour	308 (7.7)	5 (2.1)	5 (1.0)	318 (6.7)
NGO/Voluntary organisation	5 (0.1)	-	-	5 (0.1)
Any other	93 (2.3)	5 (2.1)	17 (3.3)	115 (2.4)
Non-worker/Student	16 (0.4)	2 (0.8)	-	18 (0.4)
Total	4,017 (100)	243 (100)	515 (100)	4,775 (100)

Note: Figures in brackets are percentages.

TABLE 4.7a
Secondary Occupation of Panchayat Members

Occupation	GP	TP	ZP	Overall
No secondary Occupation	2,476 (61.6)	158 (65.0)	299 (58.1)	2,933 (61.4)
Agriculture	4 (0.1)	1 (0.4)	1 (0.2)	6 (0.1)
Craftsmen	18 (0.4)	-	-	18 (0.4)
Self-employment	71 (1.8)	6 (2.5)	12 (2.3)	89 (1.9)
Domestic work	625 (15.6)	32 (13.2)	48 (9.3)	705 (14.8)
Petty trader	148 (3.7)	5 (2.1)	28 (5.4)	181 (3.8)
Cottage industry/ (Weaving/Spinning)	39 (1.0)	-	10 (1.9)	49 (1.0)
Teacher/Lecturer	6 (0.1)	-	1 (0.2)	7 (0.1)
Contractor	61 (1.5)	4 (1.6)	13 (2.5)	78 (1.6)
Full-time party work	76 (1.9)	17 (7.0)	45 (8.7)	138 (2.9)
Agricultural labour	320 (8.0)	6 (2.5)	3 (0.6)	329 (6.9)
NGO/Voluntary organisation	13 (0.3)	4 (1.6)	7 (1.4)	24 (0.5)
Any other	160 (4.0)	10 (4.1)	48 (9.3)	218 (4.7)
Total	4,017 (100)	243 (100)	515 (100)	4,775 (100)

Note: Figures in brackets are percentages.

ECONOMIC PROFILE OF THE MEMBERS

It is generally said that the economic elite controls the levers of state power. In the rural context feudal interests dominate the scene. It was therefore necessary to probe into the economic status of the elected members.

Annual Income

Table 4.8, which deals with income distribution, reveals that nearly 55.5 per cent of the elected members have an annual income of less than Rs. 10,000. Only about 11 per cent of the members received an annual income of more than Rs. 50,000. But there are considerable differences between the three tiers. While nearly 60 per cent of the members belong to Rs.10,000 and below groups at the gram panchayat level, the percentage drops to 37 at the taluk panchayat and 31.3 at the zilla panchayat levels. The reverse is the case in high-income groups. The percentage of members with an annual income of over Rs. 50,000 is higher at the zilla panchayat (27.5) than the taluk panchayat (11.2) and gram panchayat (8.7) levels. This shows the domination of high-income groups at the zilla panchayat level.

Sources of Income

The main sources of income of the elected members were also studied. The data, presented in Table 4.9, shows that agriculture is the main source of income for a majority of the members at all levels. However, the share of this source is larger at the zilla panchayat than at the other two levels. While 420 out of the 515 members (81.6 per cent) at zilla panchayat level depend on agriculture as their main source of income, at gram panchayat level the percentage drops at 67.7. For 15 per cent of the gram panchayat members wage labour is their main source of income; the percentage at the taluk panchayat and zilla panchayat levels is 6.6 and 3.1, respectively. This explains the earlier observation that a large section of the gram panchayat members belong to lower-income groups. Small business, contract work and government service are the other sources of income.

TABLE 4.8
Income Distribution of Panchayat Members

Level of Income	GP	TP	ZP	Overall
Below 5,000	1,272 (31.7)	36 (14.8)	51 (9.9)	1,359 (28.5)
5,000 to 10,000	1,123 (28.0)	55 (22.6)	110 (21.4)	1,288 (27.0)
10,000 to 15,000	351 (8.7)	37 (15.2)	40 (7.8)	428 (9.0)
15,000 to 25,000	462 (11.5)	43 (17.7)	77 (7.8)	582 (12.2)
25,000 to 50,000	462 (11.5)	46 (18.9)	95 (18.4)	603 (12.6)
50,000 to 75,000	132 (3.3)	8 (3.3)	45 (8.7)	185 (3.9)
75,000 to 1,00,000	128 (3.2)	13 (5.8)	55 (10.7)	196 (4.1)
1 lakh to 2 lakhs	56 (1.4)	5 (2.1)	29 (5.6)	90 (1.9)
Above 2 lakhs	31 (0.8)	-	13 (2.5)	44 (0.9)
Total	4,017 (100)	243 (100)	515 (100)	4,775 (100)

Note: Figures in brackets are percentages.

TABLE 4.9
Income Sources of Panchayat Members

Source of Income	GP	TP	ZP	Overall
Agriculture	2,721 (67.7)	186 (76.5)	420 (81.6)	3,327 (69.7)
Coolie (agriculture wage labourer)	598 (14.9)	16 (6.6)	16 (3.1)	630 (13.2)
Business	273 (6.8)	18 (7.4)	33 (6.4)	324 (6.8)
Rent	11 (0.3)	1 (0.4)	2 (0.4)	14 (0.3)
Employment/ Service	118 (2.9)	8 (3.3)	20 (3.9)	146 (3.1)
Beedi rolling	19 (0.5)	1 (0.4)	2 (0.4)	22 (0.5)
Contract work	36 (0.9)	1 (0.4)	1 (0.2)	38 (0.8)
Professional	14 (0.3)	1 (0.4)	14 (2.7)	29 (0.6)
Artisan	20 (0.5)	-	-	20 (0.4)
Fishery/Poultry/ Sheep rearing	22 (0.5)	-	-	22 (0.5)
Others	114 (2.8)	6 (2.5)	5 (1.0)	125 (2.6)
Self-employment	71 (1.8)	5 (2.1)	2 (0.4)	78 (1.6)
Total	4,017 (100)	243 (100)	515 (100)	4,775 (100)

Note: Figures in brackets are percentages.

Ownership of Land and Assets

Land is an important productive resource in rural areas. Access to land is an important index of political and economic clout in villages. Land and asset ownership of the members are presented in the Tables 4.10 and 4.10a

The data reveal that a majority of the elected members own land. Only 19.2 per cent of the members are landless. However, not everyone belonging to the landowning class possesses land with irrigation facilities which assures more income than the dry land. Among the elected members 45.8 per cent own irrigated land, and 52 per cent dry land. Only 17 per cent own land grown with high value commercial crops like coffee, banana, rubber, etc. Disaggregated analysis reveals that landlessness is higher among gram panchayat members (21.2 per cent) compared to taluk panchayat (9.9 per cent) and zilla panchayat (8 per cent) members. This fits with our earlier observation that wage labourers constitute a larger fraction among members at the gram panchayat level. Even among the landowning class, the share of members with irrigated land is higher at the taluk panchayat and zilla panchayat levels than at the gram panchayat level. Same is the case with land under plantation crops.

Table 4.10
Land Ownership of Panchayat Members

Type of Land	GP	TP	ZP	Overall
Landless	852 (21.2)	24 (9.9)	41 (8.0)	917 (19.2)
Irrigated land	1,733 (43.1)	148 (60.9)	305 (59.2)	2,186 (45.8)
Dry land	2,039 (50.8)	134 (55.1)	326 (63.3)	2,499 (52.3)
Plantation field (coffee, banana, rubber etc.)	630 (15.7)	61 (25.1)	139 (27.0)	830 (17.4)
Others	27 (0.7)	1 (0.4)	5 (1.0)	33 (0.7)

Note: Figures in brackets are percentages.

TABLE 4.10a
Asset Ownership of Panchayat Members

Assets		GP	TP	ZP	Overall
Land	Yes	3,165 (78.8)	219 (90.1)	474 (92.0)	3,858 (80.8)
	No	852 (11.2)	24 (9.9)	41 (8.0)	917 (19.2)
Livestock	Yes	2,523 (62.8)	165 (67.9)	379 (73.6)	3,067 (64.2)
	No	1,494 (37.2)	78 (32.1)	136 (26.4)	1,708 (35.8)
Tractor	Yes	237 (5.9)	39 (16.0)	107 (20.8)	383 (8.0)
	No	3,780 (94.1)	204 (84.0)	408 (79.2)	4,392 (92.0)
Tiller	Yes	135 (3.4)	18 (7.4)	46 (8.9)	199 (4.2)
	No	3,882 (96.6)	125 (92.6)	469 (91.1)	4,576 (95.8)
Pumpset	Yes	1,197 (19.8)	111 (45.7)	299 (58.1)	1,607 (37.7)
	No	2,820 (70.2)	132 (54.3)	216 (41.9)	3,168 (66.3)
Other agricultural assets	Yes	985 (14.5)	68 (28.0)	201 (39.0)	1,254 (26.3)
	No	3,032 (75.5)	175 (72.0)	314 (61.0)	3,521 (73.7)
Vehicles	Yes	869 (11.6)	115 (47.3)	279 (54.2)	1,263 (26.5)
	No	3,148 (78.4)	128 (52.7)	236 (45.8)	3,512 (73.5)

Table 4.10a contd...

TABLE 4.10a *contd.*

Assets		GP	TP	ZP	Overall
Phone	Yes	362 (9.0)	65 (26.7)	220 (42.7)	647 (13.5)
	No	3,655 (91.0)	178 (73.3)	295 (57.3)	4,128 (86.5)
Radio/TV	Yes	2,835 (70.6)	208 (85.6)	473 (91.8)	3,516 (73.6)
	No	1,182 (19.4)	35 (14.4)	42 (8.2)	1,259 (26.4)
House	Own	3,880 (96.6)	227 (93.4)	485 (94.2)	4,592 (96.2)
	Rented	137 (3.4)	16 (6.6)	30 (5.8)	183 (3.8)
Total		4,017	243	515	4,775

Note: Figures in brackets are percentages.

EXPOSURE TO MASS MEDIA

Reading/Watching/Listening

Exposure to mass media plays an important role in educating members about their rights and responsibilities. Exposure in the form of the habit of reading newspapers, watching TV, and listening to radio regularly is analysed in Tables 4.11 and 4.11a.

Among elected members on the whole only 67 per cent read newspapers and magazines. The habit of reading newspaper appears to be almost universal among the members at the zilla panchayat level (95 per cent). It is considerably less (63 per cent) among the Gram Panchayat members. This may be due to their lower literacy rates and dependence on wage labour for livelihood which leaves very little time and opportunity to read newspapers. An analysis of the habit of listening to radio/watching TV also gives a similar picture.

TABLE 4.11
Reading Newspapers/Magazines

Read Newspapers/ Magazines	GP	TP	ZP	Overall
Yes	2,523 (62.8)	213 (87.7)	489 (95.0)	3,225 (67.5)
No	1,494 (37.2)	30 (12.3)	26 (5.0)	1,550 (32.5)
Total	4,017 (100)	243 (100)	515 (100)	4,775 (100)

Note: Figures in brackets are percentages.

TABLE 4.11a
Listening to Radio/Watching TV

Radio/TV	GP	TP	ZP	Overall
Yes	2,920 (72.7)	210 (86.4)	477 (92.6)	3,607 (75.5)
No	1,097 (27.3)	33 (13.6)	38 (7.4)	1,168 (24.5)
Total	4,017 (100)	243 (100)	515 (100)	4,775 (100)

Note: Figures in brackets are the percentages.

Preferences for Different Programmes

Table 4.12 demonstrates that news is the most popular and preferred programme at all the panchayat levels. It also shows the extent of interest in public and political issues among panchayat members. Although the percentage of gram panchayat members watching/listening to news is considerably less than other two categories, the figure is substantial in itself. The programmes which evoked least interest among members were legal, sports and cultural.

TABLE 4.12
Programmes Generally Preferred

Programmes	GP	TP	ZP	Overall
Do not listen/watch	1,098 (27.3)	33 (13.6)	38 (7.4)	1,169 (24.5)
News	2,556 (63.6)	191 (78.6)	447 (86.8)	3,194 (66.9)
Legal	46 (1.1)	4 (1.6)	14 (2.7)	64 (1.3)
Agricultural	448 (11.2)	22 (9.1)	71 (13.8)	541 (11.3)
Entertainment	326 (8.1)	18 (7.4)	33 (6.4)	377 (7.9)
Women-related programmes	111 (2.8)	8 (3.3)	29 (5.6)	148 (3.1)
Political programmes/ Parliament news	236 (5.9)	18 (7.4)	64 (12.4)	318 (6.7)
Sports	35 (0.9)	4 (1.6)	10 (1.9)	49 (1.0)
Cultural	56 (1.4)	6 (2.5)	5 (1.0)	67 (1.4)
Serials/Films/Songs	649 (16.2)	44 (18.1)	80 (15.5)	773 (16.2)
All Kannada programmes	97 (2.4)	6 (2.5)	9 (1.7)	120 (2.5)
Others	388 (9.7)	36 (14.8)	96 (18.6)	513 (10.7)

Note: Figures in brackets are percentages.

POLITICAL PROFILE OF MEMBERS

Affiliation to Political Parties

Participation in political party activities is important because it leads to political socialisation and education. It also gives members the training and confidence to enter politics and one cannot deny the motivating role of the party in making of leaders. Table 4.13 reveals the party affiliations of the respondents.

The gram panchayat elections were held on non-party basis. However, grouping of members on political party-lines was evident. During our study we found that only 7.3 per cent of the respondents (gram panchayat members) reported that they were independent, having no affiliation to any of the political parties. This means political parties have taken roots even at the lowest level – the gram panchayat level – and those who contest or get elected do not hide their political party affiliation.

At the taluk and zilla panchayat levels the political parties officially participated in the elections. The Janata Dal, in general, is the most preferred party at all the three levels. However, among the respondents a higher percentage of the Gram Panchayat members reported that they align themselves with the Congress(I). But the Congress(I) at the taluk and zilla panchayat levels had only 21.8 and 10.6 per cent respectively.

The BJP had gained relatively more support at taluk panchayat level. At the taluk level 10.3 per cent of the respondents said they were BJP members. Their percentage at the gram panchayats and zilla panchayats were only 7.1 and 6.4 respectively. Only 1.2 per cent at the taluk panchayat level and 1.4 per cent at the zilla panchayat level said they were independent and not affiliated to any political party.

Though at the village level political parties were not given official recognition and elections were conducted on a non-party basis, respondents confessed their party affiliation. Data also support this since the number of independents was meagre. Orientation towards left parties such as the CPI and CPI(M) is rather negligible.

TABLE 4.13
Political Party Affiliation of Members

Party	GP	TP	ZP	Overall
Janata Dal	1,658 (41.3)	156 (64.2)	360 (69.9)	2,174 (45.5)
Congress(I)	1583 (39.4)	53 (21.8)	101 (19.6)	1737 (36.4)
BJP	286 (7.1)	25 (10.3)	33 (6.4)	344 (7.2)
KCP	82 (2.0)	-	4 (.8)	86 (1.8)
BSP	6 (.1)	2 (.8)	-	8 (.2)
CPI	1 (.0)	1 (.4)	1 (.2)	3 (.1)
CPI(M)	4 (.1)	1 (.4)	2 (.4)	7 (.1)
KRRS	72 (1.8)	2 (.8)	4 (.8)	78 (1.6)
Independent	292 (7.3)	3 (1.2)	7 (1.4)	302 (6.3)
RPI	7 (.2)	-	-	7 (.1)
Vatal Kannda Party	10 (.2)	-	2 (.4)	12 (.3)
MES	16 (.4)	-	1 (.2)	17 (.4)
Total	4,017	243	515	4,775

Note: Figures in brackets are percentages.

Although political parties' participation in panchayats is a much debated question, since the West Bengal panchayat elections of 1978, officially political parties have been entering local bodies. In Karnataka, this election saw the emergence of smaller local parties as well. In particular, KRRS made its presence felt – their share of the total membership in Karnataka panchayats is 1.6 per cent.

Previous Political Experience

Previous political experience of other family members of the respondent and their own experience in a different position is presented in Tables 4.14 and 4.15 respectively. Previous political experience of other family members appears to be substantial (53 per cent) at the zilla panchayat level. At the level of gram panchayat and taluk panchayat, the political experience of other family members of respondents were found to be 24.8 per cent and 39.9 per cent respectively. This shows that the zilla panchayat members are more exposed to political matters. At the gram panchayat level there are more new entrants. An analysis of the previous political experience of the members shows that some of them had worked at the mandal/zilla parishad levels prior to their present position.

TABLE 4.14
Previous Political Experience of Family

Response	GP	TP	ZP	Overall
Yes	996 (24.8)	97 (39.9)	277 (53.8)	1,370 (28.7)
No	3,021 (75.2)	146 (60.1)	238 (46.2)	3,405 (71.3)
Total	4,017 (100)	243 (100)	515 (100)	4,775 (100)

Note: Figures in brackets are percentages.

TABLE 4.15
Previous Political Experience of Members

Previous experience	GP	TP	ZP	Overall
No previous experience	3,627 (90.3)	188 (77.4)	343 (66.6)	4,158 (87.1)
MP	-	-	1 (.02)	1 (.02)
MLA/MLC	1 (.02)	-	1 (.02)	2 (.04)
Mandal/Zilla parishad	345 (8.6)	41 (16.9)	140 (27.2)	526 (11.0)
Taluk board	19 (.5)	2 (.8)	32 (6.2)	53 (1.1)
Other	136 (3.4)	28 (11.5)	71 (13.8)	235 (4.9)

Note: Figures in brackets are percentages.

Involvement of Present and Previous Generation in Politics

The involvement of any family member in organisations or movements of social welfare, service or political orientation invariably affects the other members of the family.

The involvement of brothers, sisters and spouses from among the present generation, and father, mother and others belonging to an older generation, in socio-political activity is analysed in Tables 4.16 and 4.16a.

Among the zilla panchayat members, 5.4 per cent have their brothers and another 5.4 per cent their spouses active in politics. These percentages are lower at the gram panchayat level. But in the case of involvement of the older generation, 19 per cent of the zilla panchayat members compared to 7.6 per cent of the gram panchayat and 15.6 per cent of the taluk panchayat had their fathers in politics. This supports our earlier observation that a majority of the gram panchayat members are new entrants.

TABLE 4.16
Involvement of Older Generation in Politics

Previous Generation	GP	TP	ZP	Overall
Nobody	3,564 (88.7)	200 (82.3)	404 (78.5)	4,168 (87.3)
Father	307 (7.6)	38 (15.6)	96 (18.6)	441 (9.2)
Mother	38 (.9)	4 (1.6)	9 (1.7)	51 (1.1)
Other family members	183 (4.6)	15 (6.2)	48 (9.3)	246 (5.2)

Note: Figures in brackets are percentages.

TABLE 4.16a
Involvement of Present Generation in Politics

Present Generation	GP	TP	ZP	Overall
Nobody	3,813 (94.9)	221 (91.0)	458 (89.0)	4,492 (94.1)
Brother	78 (1.9)	3 (1.2)	28 (5.4)	109 (2.3)
Sister	11 (.3)	-	4 (.8)	15 (.3)
Husband/Wife	86 (2.1)	14 (5.8)	28 (5.4)	128 (2.7)
Other family members	43 (1.1)	5 (2.1)	9 (1.7)	57 (1.2)

Note: Figures in brackets are percentages.

A detailed enquiry into the leaders' family involvement in political activities revealed that more than 70 per cent of them did not have any such background. It was also found that the leaders themselves had not enjoyed any such positions before.

Ideological Commitment of Members

The ideology of the elected members at all the three levels is presented in Table 4.17.

TABLE 4.17
Ideology of Members

Ideology	GP	TP	ZP	Overall
Dalit	341 (8.5)	15 (6.2)	19 (3.7)	375 (7.9)
Social justice	2,090 (52.0)	154 (63.4)	324 (62.9)	2,568 (53.8)
Hindutva	145 (3.6)	10 (4.1)	11 (2.1)	166 (3.5)
Socialistic	209 (5.2)	13 (5.3)	32 (6.2)	254 (5.3)
Gandhian	408 (10.2)	24 (9.9)	46 (8.9)	478 (10.0)
Any other	49 (1.2)	-	11 (2.1)	60 (1.3)
No ideology	538 (13.4)	20 (8.2)	52 (10.1)	610 (12.8)
No information/ Don't know	237 (5.9)	7 (2.9)	20 (3.9)	264 (5.5)
Total	4,017 (100)	243 (100)	515 (100)	4,775 (100)

Note: Figures in brackets are percentages.

Ideological commitment of the members will have an impact on the priorities and functioning of the PRIs. An enquiry into this aspect revealed that a majority of the elected members (54 per cent) are committed to social justice. Apart from this, Gandhian principles is another important ideology of nearly 10 per cent of the members. At a micro level, the percentage of gram panchayat members committed to social justice is smaller than the members of other categories (see Table 4.17). Ten to thirteen per cent of the members at all levels do not seem to follow any given ideology.

Priorities of Elected Members for Next Five Years

The perception of the elected members about local problems and the priority accorded to them are vital. Priorities in the next five years are shown in the Tables 4.18 and 4.18a.

TABLE 4.18
First Priority for Next Five Years

Priority - I	GP	TP	ZP	Overall
Education	2,615 (64.1)	200 (82.3)	428 (83.1)	3,243 (67.9)
Family planning/ Welfare	479 (11.9)	17 (7.0)	24 (4.7)	520 (10.9)
Health	469 (11.7)	20 (8.2)	31 (6.0)	520 (10.9)
Sanitation	257 (6.4)	5 (2.1)	11 (2.1)	273 (5.7)
Other	89 (2.2)	1 (.4)	13 (2.5)	103 (2.2)
No priorities/ No information	108 (2.7)		8 (1.6)	116 (2.4)
Total	4,017 (100)	243 (100)	515 (100)	4,775 (100)

Note: Figures in brackets are percentages.

TABLE 4.18a
Second Priority for Next Five Years

Priority - II	GP	TP	ZP	Overall
Family planning	457 (11.4)	43 (17.7)	76 (14.8)	576 (12.1)
Health	674 (16.8)	59 (24.3)	124 (24.1)	857 (17.9)
Sanitation	2,287 (56.9)	118 (48.6)	239 (46.4)	2,645 (55.4)
Other	343 (8.5)	19 (7.8)	51 (9.9)	412 (8.6)
No 2nd priority/ No information	256 (6.4)	4 (1.6)	25 (4.9)	285 (6.0)
Total	4,017 (100)	243 (100)	515 (100)	4,775 (100)

Note: Figures in brackets are percentages.

An analysis of the table 4.18 shows that for a majority of the members (67.9 per cent), education is the most important issue. Family planning and health are the other important priorities. However, there are differences in priorities at the three levels. Though education is given the highest priority by members at all levels the percentage at the gram panchayat level is considerably lower compared to the other two levels. Family planning, health and sanitation are given first priority by more members at the gram panchayat level. But these are given second highest priority by elected members of the taluk and zilla panchayats. Many of the respondents were thus concerned about local welfare issues.

Motivational Forces

The agents responsible for arousal of political interest of the elected members are analysed here in Table 4.19.

TABLE 4.19

Agents which Motivated Members to Contest Elections

Motivator	GP	TP	ZP	Overall
Family Members	1,005 (25.02)	69 (28.40)	146 (28.35)	1,220 (25.55)
Friends	1,103 (27.46)	87 (35.80)	172 (33.40)	1,362 (28.52)
Zamindar	185 (4.61)	5 (2.06)	16 (3.11)	206 (4.31)
Farmers/Labourers	1,045 (26.01)	40 (16.46)	97 (18.83)	1,182 (24.75)
Professional organisations	22 (0.55)	4 (1.65)	4 (0.78)	30 (0.63)
Interest in social work	405 (10.08)	32 (13.17)	92 (17.86)	529 (11.08)
Caste/Religion	189 (4.71)	6 (2.47)	21 (4.08)	216 (4.52)
Self	1,135 (28.25)	73 (30.04)	158 (30.68)	1,366 (28.61)
Community	1,168 (29.08)	56 (23.05)	136 (26.41)	1,360 (28.48)
Others	116 2.89	6 2.47	23 4.47	145 3.04

Note: Figures in brackets are percentages.

The data show that percentage of members motivated by self (28.61), family members (25.55), friends (28.52), and village community (28.48) are more or less equal. At the gram panchayat level fellow farmers and agricultural labourers appear to be more influential in motivating the members (26.01 per cent).

Participation in Associations/Organisations

Participation in various associations and organisations was another feature of the profile of members which was examined.

From Table 4.20 it appears that more zilla panchayat members are participating in some association or organisation than members at taluk and gram panchayat members. While 58 per cent of the gram panchayat members are not associated with any organisation, only 32 per cent of the zilla panchayat members are without any organisational association.

TABLE 4.20
Participation in Associations/Organisations

Organisation/ Association	GP	TP	ZP	Overall
No participation	2,323 (57.8)	104 (42.8)	165 (32.0)	2,592 (54.3)
Social welfare organisation	157 (3.9)	30 (12.3)	73 (14.2)	260 (5.4)
Youth association	485 (12.1)	49 (20.2)	83 (16.1)	617 (12.9)
Women association	269 (6.7)	24 (9.9)	70 (13.6)	363 (7.6)
Caste association	376 (9.4)	35 (14.4)	84 (16.3)	495 (10.4)
Farmer association	255 (6.3)	27 (11.1)	61 (11.8)	343 (7.2)
Trader association/ Business association	132 (3.3)	11 (4.5)	51 (9.9)	194 (4.1)
Professional association	27 (.7)	6 (2.5)	8 (1.6)	41 (.9)

Table 4.20 Contd...

TABLE 4.20 *Contd.*

Organisation/ Association	GP	TP	ZP	Overall
Trade union	37 (.7)	4 (1.6)	13 (2.5)	54 (1.1)
Student union	90 (2.2)	15 (6.2)	30 (5.8)	135 (2.8)
Cultural/Religious association	203 (5.1)	25 (10.3)	34 (6.6)	262 (5.5)
Lions/Rotary club	33 (.8)	5 (2.1)	26 (5.0)	64 (1.3)
Cooperative societies	693 (17.3)	43 (17.7)	143 (27.8)	879 (18.4)
Educational institution	7 (.2)	-	2 (.3)	9 (.2)
Any other	80 (2.0)	3 (1.2)	23 (4.5)	106 (2.2)

Note: Figures in brackets are percentages.

A cooperative society is the main kind of organisation with which a majority of the members at all levels are associated. Youth and caste associations are of some importance. Only a small percentage were members of cultural or religious associations. It thus appears that people prefer socially and development-oriented associations.

Membership in Standing Committees

These committees are miniature councils to which some specific tasks are referred or committed. They ensure wider participation in decision-making on the part of the panchayat members. They are emerging as an important component of the local government system. Data on membership in various committees by education level are shown in Table 4.21.

TABLE 4.21
Level of Education by Membership in Standing Committees

Level of Education	PC	SJ	AC	GS	FA	EH	AI	NF	NA
Illiterate	29 (4.6)	48 (5.8)	23 (6.6)	1 (2.0)	1 (1.1)	-	-	104 (10.0)	253 (14.8)
Literate	86 (13.7)	94 (11.4)	49 (14.0)	-	2 (2.2)	-	-	152 (14.6)	255 (14.9)
Primary	85 (13.6)	99 (12.0)	33 (9.4)	3 (5.9)	8 (8.6)	-	-	162 (15.6)	219 (12.8)
Higher primary	116 (18.5)	165 (20.1)	71 (20.2)	5 (9.8)	9 (9.7)	2 (4.9)	6 (16.2)	192 (18.5)	318 (18.6)
Secondary	164 (26.2)	228 (27.8)	87 (24.8)	18 (35.3)	35 (37.7)	10 (24.4)	11 (29.7)	266 (25.6)	380 (22.1)
PUC	57 (9.1)	73 (8.9)	30 (8.5)	7 (13.7)	9 (9.7)	8 (19.5)	7 (18.9)	55 (5.3)	105 (6.1)
Degree	74 (11.8)	78 (9.5)	47 (13.4)	10 (19.6)	22 (23.7)	15 (36.6)	10 (27.0)	82 (7.9)	132 (7.7)

Table 4.21 Contd...

TABLE 4.21 *Contd.*

Level of Education	PC	SJ	AC	GS	FA	EH	AI	NF	NA
Postgraduation	4 (.6)	7 (.9)	3 (.9)	3 (5.9)	3 (3.2)	1 (2.4)	1 (2.7)	5 (.5)	10 (.6)
Law	4 (.6)	13 (1.6)	1 (.3)	2 (3.9)	1 (1.1)	3 (7.3)	1 (2.7,	5 (.5)	14 (.8)
Engineering	-	5 (.5)	2 (.6)	1 (2.0)	-	1 (2.4)	-	1 (.1)	6 (.4)
Diploma	4 (.6)	5 (.6)	2 (.6)	1 (2.0)	1 (1.1)	1 (2.4)	-	8 (.8)	12 (.7)
Medicine	1 (.2)	3 (.4)	1 (.3)	-	1 (1.1)	-	-	2 (.2)	2 (.1)
B Ed/M Ed	-	3 (.4)	-	-	-	-	1 (2.7)	3 (.3)	4 (.2)
Any other	2 (.3)	1 (.1)	2 (.6)	-	1 (1.1)	-	-	3 (.3)	4 (.2)
Total	626 (13.1)	822 (17.2)	351 (7.4)	51 (1.1)	93 (1.9)	41 (.9)	37 (.8)	1,040 (21.8)	1,714 (35.9)

Note: Figures in brackets are percentages. PC: Production Committee; SJ: Social Justice Committee; AC: Amenities Committee; GS: General Standing Committee; FA: Finance & Audit Committee; EH: Education & Health Committe; AI: Agriculture & Industry Committee; NF: Not formed any committee; NA: Not aware.

Some of the respondents were members of various committees of the panchayats. In some panchayats, (21.8 per cent) committees which are statutory bodies, have not yet been formed. It should be noted that even though committees are an integral part of the system, many educated members (16.6 per cent) have expressed their ignorance about the committees and their functioning.

AWARENESS ABOUT THE PANCHAYATI RAJ SYSTEM

The perception of members regarding decentralised governance was also elicited. Open-ended questions were used. The answers given by the respondents were recorded and processed.

Most of the respondents would like panchayats to be vested with more powers. They felt although PRIs are important for rural development, they face major financial constraints as the government grants are not sufficient. Reservation was appreciated, but a small percentage of the members were of the view that presidentship should not be reserved. And wherever it is necessary to reserve, education should be the criterion for selection. Some members were of the opinion that the earlier mandal system was more sensitive to the local needs and hence more effective.

It was also observed that some of the respondents did not respond to this question. It appears they still have not been able to grasp the working of the panchayati raj system. This is not encouraging because the success of the system depends on the political maturity and understanding of the leaders.

Chapter V

Background of Adhyakshas and Upadhyakshas

This chapter analyses the socio-economic background, ideologies, priorities and motivational forces of panchayat leaders, namely adhyakshas and upadhyakshas. Since they head the panchayats and their role is more important than that of ordinary members, a separate analysis of their background is warranted. The success of the panchayati raj institution will depend largely on the quality of this leadership. The analysis was carried out both at the aggregate level and for each tier, i.e., gram, taluk and zilla.

OVERALL VIEW OF ADHYAKSHAS AND UPADHYAKSHAS

Of the 4,775 elected members who were interviewed, 599 were adhyakshas, 532 were upadhyakshas, and 3,664 were members. Tables 5.1 and 5.1a give the distribution of the members according to gender and position.

TABLE 5.1
Genderwise Break-up of Members by Position in Panchayat.

Position	Men	Women	Total
Adhyaksha	340 (56.8)	259 (43.2)	599 (12.5)
Upadhyaksha	293 (55.1)	239 (44.9)	532 (11.1)
Members	2,211 (60.7)	1,433 (39.3)	3,644 (76.3)
Total	2,844 (59.6)	1,931 (40.4)	4,775 (100)

Note: Figures in brackets are percentages.

The data show that among the adhyakshas, 56.8 per cent are men and 43.2 per cent are women. Among the upadhyakshas, 55.1 per cent are men and 44.9 per cent women. Of the total respondents thus 12.5 per cent are adhyakshas and 11.1 upadhyakshas.

TABLE 5.1a
Distribution of Members according to Position and Gender at Different Panchayat Levels

Position	GP		TP		ZP	
	Men	Women	Men	Women	Men	Women
Adhyaksha (A)	314 (56.4)	243 (43.6)	14 (60.9)	9 (39.1)	12 (63.2)	7 (36.8)
Upadhyaksha (U)	267 (54.7)	221 (45.3)	14 (58.3)	10 (41.7)	12 (60.0)	8 (40.0)
Members (M)	1,793 (60.3)	1,179 (39.7)	117 (59.7)	79 (40.3)	301 (63.2)	175 (36.8)
Total	2,374 (59.1)	1,643 (40.9)	145 (59.7)	98 (40.3)	325 (63.1)	190 (36.9)

Note: Figures in brackets are percentages.

SOCIAL PROFILE

Age

It is evident from the Table 5.2 that a majority of the adhyakshas and upadhyakshas are below 40 years of age. A substantial number also fall between 41 to 50 years of age. It is evident that women leaders are relatively younger.

Caste

Caste plays an important role in our society, particularly in rural areas. Table 5.3 shows the castewise distribution of the elected members both at the aggregate and disaggregated levels according to their position in the panchayat. This analysis gives an idea about the role of caste in influencing leadership.

TABLE 5.2
Distribution of Adhyakshas and Upadhyakshas by Age and Gender

Age of	Men		Women	
Respondents	A	U	A	U
Upto 25 years	11 (3.2)	6 (2.0)	30 (11.6)	18 (7.5)
26 to 30 years	35 (10.3)	34 (11.6)	44 (17.0)	47 (19.7)
31 to 35 years	54 (15.9)	50 (17.1)	62 (23.9)	60 (25.1)
36 to 40 years	88 (25.9)	72 (24.6)	41 (15.8)	40 (16.7)
41 to 50 years	106 (31.2)	95 (32.4)	57 (22.0)	52 (21.8)
51 to 60 years	33 (9.7)	28 (9.6)	20 (7.7)	18 (7.5)
61 to 70 years	11 (3.2)	6 (2.0)	3 (1.2)	4 (1.7)
71 years & above	2 (.6)	2 (.7)	2 (.8)	
Total	340	293	259	239

Note: (1) A - Adhyaksha U - Upadhyaksha
(2) Figures in brackets are percentages.

The domination of BCs in all positions is fairly pronounced. The representation of SC adhyakshas of gram panchayats in our survey is only 13.6 per cent (see Table 5.4). It is lower than the prescribed reservation quota (15 per cent) for them. The reason for this lower percentage is due to the random selection of the sample units for the gram panchayat adhyakshas and the upadhyakshas in this study. However, the total SC members' composition is well within their prescribed reservation limits.

TABLE 5.3
Castewise Distribution of Panchayat Members according to Position

Caste	Adhyaksha	Upadhyaksha	Member
Scheduled Caste	80 (12.4)	86 (16.2)	569 (15.6)
Backward Caste	262 (43.8)	210 (39.5)	1466 (40.2)
Forward Caste	23 (3.9)	18 (3.4)	155 (4.3)
Scheduled Tribe	61 (10.2)	54 (10.2)	321 (8.7)
Others	173 (28.9)	164 (30.8)	1,132 (31.3)
Total	599 (100.00)	532 (100.00)	3,644 (100.00)

Note: Figures in brackets are percentages.

Castewise Distribution of Respondents at All Three Levels

The disaggregated picture of the caste groups (Table 5.4) shows that more offices of the adhyakshas at the taluk and zilla panchayat levels have gone in favour of the Backward Castes. The SC representation is higher among adhyakshas at the gram and zilla panchayat levels. Same is the case with the ST category.

Educational Status

Table 5.5 shows the educational status of the adhyakshas, upadhyaksha and members at all levels. The data reveal two things clearly. First, illiteracy is higher among the upadhyakshas and members. Second, the illiteracy rates of female members are considerably higher at all positions, particularly among members. Compared to 20.6 per cent of the male adhyakshas, only 3.1 per cent of the female adhyakshas are graduates.

TABLE 5.4
Castewise Distribution of Members at Three Panchayat Levels

Caste	Gram Panchayat			Taluk Panchayat			Zilla Panchayat		
	A	U	M	A	U	M	A	U	M
Forward Caste	20 (3.6)	16 (3.3)	126 (4.2)	2 (8.6)	2 (8.4)	9 (4.6)	1 (5.3)	-	20 (4.2)
Backward Caste	243 (26.7)	190 (38.9)	1,141 (32.5)	12 (52.0)	11 (45.8)	85 (43.4)	7 (36.9)	9 (45.0)	240 (50.4)
Scheduled Caste	76 (13.6)	82 (16.9)	501 (16.9)	1 (4.3)	2 (8.3)	23 (11.7)	3 (15.8)	2 (10.0)	45 (9.5)
Scheduled Tribe	58 (10.4)	49 (10.0)	252 (8.4)	1 (4.3)	2 (8.4)	23 (11.7)	2 (10.6)	3 (15.0)	47 (9.8)
Others	160 (28.8)	151 (30.9)	952 (32.0)	7 (30.4)	7 (29.1)	56 (28.6)	6 (31.6)	6 (30.0)	124 (26.0)
Total	557 (100)	488 (100)	2,972 (100)	23 (100)	24 (100)	196 (100)	19 (100)	20 (100)	476 (100)

Note: (1) A - Adhyaksha U - Upadhyaksha M - Member
(2) Figures in brackets are percentages.

TABLE 5.5
Educational Status of Panchayat Members

Literacy	Adhyaksha		Upadhyaksha		Members	
	Male	Female	Male	Female	Male	Female
Illiterate	1 (0.3)	24 (9.3)	13 (4.4)	41 (17.2)	104 (4.7)	276 (19.3)
Read & write	15 (4.4)	64 (24.7)	30 (10.2)	47 (19.7)	186 (8.4)	296 (20.7)
Primary	40 (11.8)	38 (14.7)	36 (12.3)	41 (17.2)	247 (11.2)	207 (14.4)
Higher primary	56 (16.5)	71 (27.4)	52 (17.7)	43 (18.0)	402 (18.2)	260 (18.1)
Secondary	41 (12.1)	24 (9.3)	33 (11.3)	20 (8.4)	265 (12.0)	123 (8.6)
SSLC	74 (21.8)	17 (6.6)	61 (20.8)	28 (11.7)	369 (16.7)	144 (10.0)
PUC	29 (8.5)	12 (4.6)	29 (9.9)	9 (3.8)	215 (9.7)	57 (4.0)
Degree	70 (20.6)	8 (3.1)	31 (10.5)	7 (2.9)	378 (17.2)	57 (4.0)
Postgraduate	8 (2.4)	-	4 (1.4)	2 (0.8)	17 (0.8)	6 (0.4)
Diploma	5 (1.5)	-	4 (1.4)	1 (0.4)	22 (1.0)	2 (0.1)
Others	1 (0.3)	1 (0.4)	-	-	6 (0.3)	5 (0.3)
Total	340 (100)	259 (100)	239 (100)	239 (100)	2,211 (100)	1,433 (100)

Note: Figures in brackets are percentages.

The literacy status of adhyakshas and upadhyaksha at different panchayat levels (Table 5.6) shows that illiteracy is higher among gram panchayat members. While there are no illiterates among male members at the zilla panchayat level, 0.3 per cent of the male adhyakshas, 4.5 per cent of the male upadhyakshas, and 5.7 per cent of members at gram panchayat level are illiterate.

Illiteracy among female members is found in all the three tiers, though it is higher at the gram panchayat level. It is interesting to observe that the percentage of graduates is higher among female adhyakshas than male adhyakshas at the zilla panchayat level. The converse is true at the taluk panchayat level.

Occupational Classification

Primary and secondary occupational analysis of the adhyakshas, upadhyakshas and members (Table 5.7) shows that cultivation is the main occupation for a majority of the respondents at all levels.

This is understandable from our earlier observation that most of them own land. Domestic work constitutes the next major occupation. Another important occupation is self-employment in cottage industry, petty trade, etc. In the case of agricultural labour, the share of the adhyakshas is lower than that of upadhyakshas and members.

Looking at the main occupation of adhyakshas (Table 5.8) at all three levels, it is clear that cultivation takes first place. While few of the adhyakshas at the gram panchayat level are also agricultural labourers, this occupation is absent among the adhyakshas at the taluk and zilla panchayats levels. An interesting observation is that the percentage of adhyakshas reporting party work as their main occupation is higher at the zilla panchayat level, while it is negligible at the gram panchayat level.

TABLE 5.6
Literacy Status at Different Panchayat Levels

Literacy	Gram Panchayat				Taluk Panchayat				Zilla Panchayat			
	Adhyaksha		Upadhyaksha		Adhyaksha		Upadhyaksha		Adhyaksha		Upadhyaksha	
	Male	Female	Male	Female	Male	Female	Male	Female	Male	Female	Male	Female
Illiterate	1 (0.3)	24 (9.9)	12 (4.5)	41 (18.6)	-	-	1 (7.1)	-	-	-	-	-
Read & write	15 (4.8)	64 (26.3)	30 (11.2)	45 (20.4)	-	-	-	2 (20.0)	-	-	-	-
Primary	40 (12.7)	36 (14.8)	36 (13.5)	41 (18.6)	-	2 (22.2)	-	-	-	-	-	-
Higher primary	56 (17.8)	68 (28.0)	50 (18.7)	41 (18.6)	-	2 (22.2)	1 (7.1)	2 (20.0)	-	1 ·14.3	1 8.3	-
Secondary	40 (12.7)	24 (9.9)	30 (11.2)	17 (7.7)	-	-	2 (14.3)	2 (20.0)	1 (8.3)	-	1 (8.3)	1 (12.5)
SSLC	64 (24.4)	13 (5.3)	55 (20.6)	25 (11.3)	6 (42.9)	3 (33.3)	2 (14.3)	2 (20.0)	4 (33.3)	1 (14.3)	4 (33.3)	1 (12.5)
PUC	28 (8.9)	11 (4.5)	22 (8.2)	6 (2.7)	-	-	4 (28.6)	2 (20.0)	1 (8.3)	1 (14.3)	3 (25.0)	1 (12.5)

Table 5.6 Contd...

TABLE 5.6 *Contd.*

Literacy	Gram Panchayat				Taluk Panchayat				Zilla Panchayat			
	Adhyaksha		Upadhyaksha		Adhyaksha		Upadhyaksha		Adhyaksha		Upadhyaksha	
	Male	Female	Male	Female	Male	Female	Male	Female	Male	Female	Male	Female
Degree	60 (19.0)	2 (0.8)	24 (9.0)	5 (2.3)	6 (42.8)	2 (22.2)	4 (28.5)	-	4 (33.3)	4 (57.1)	3 (25.0)	2 (25.0)
PG	5 (1.6)	-	4 (1.5)	-	1 (7.1)	-	-	-	2 (16.7)	-	-	2 (25.0)
Diploma	4 (1.3)	-	4 (1.5)	-	1 (7.1)	-	-	-	-	-	-	1 (12.5)
Others	1 (0.3)	1 (0.4)	-	-	-	-	-	-	-	-	-	-
Total	314 (100)	243 (100)	267 (100)	221 (100)	14 (100)	9 (100)	14 (100)	10 (100)	12 (100)	7 (100)	12 (100)	8 (100)

Note: Figures in brackets are percentages.

Table 5.7
Occupation of Panchayat Members

Occupation	Main Occupation			Secondary Occupation		
	A	U	M	A	U	M
Agriculture	398 (66.4)	333 (62.6)	2,210 (60.6)	-	1 (0.2)	5 (0.1)
Self-employment	46 (7.7)	36 (6.8)	370 (10.2)	51 (8.5)	43 (8.2)	321 (8.8)
Domestic work	102 (17.0)	107 (20.1)	680 (18.7)	114 (19.0)	86 (16.2)	505 (13.9)
Salaried	3 (0.5)	1 (0.2)	8 (0.2)	2 (0.4)	5 (1.0)	24 (0.6)
Full-time party work	8 (1.3)	5 (0.9)	17 (0.5)	36 (6.0)	15 (2.8)	87 (2.4)
Agricultural labour	23 (3.8)	34 (6.4)	261 (7.2)	25 (4.2)	41 (7.7)	263 (7.7)
Non-worker	2 (0.3)	4 (0.8)	12 (0.3)	-	-	-
Other	17 (2.8)	12 (2.3)	86 (2.4)	25 (4.2)	23 (4.3)	170 (4.7)
No secondary occupation	-	-	-	346 (57.8)	318 (59.8)	2,269 (62.3)

Note: Figures in brackets are percentages.

TABLE 5.8

Occupation of Members at Three Panchayat Levels

Occupation	Gram Panchayat			Taluk Panchayat			Zilla Panchayat		
	A	U	M	A	U	M	A	U	M
Cultivation	372 (68.8)	309 (63.3)	1,788 (60.2)	1 (60.9)	12 (50.0)	117 (59.7)	12 (63.2)	12 (60.0)	305 (64.1)
Self-employed	43 (7.7)	32 (6.5)	317 (10.6)	3 (13.0)	4 (16.7)	24 (12.2)	-	-	29 (6.0)
Salaried	3 (0.5)	1 (0.2)	1 0.2	-	-	1 (0.5)	-	-	1 (0.2)
Agricultural labour	23 (4.1)	34 (7.0)	251 (8.4)	-	-	5 (2.6)	-	-	5 (1.1)
Party worker	5 (0.9)	3 (0.6)	11 (0.4)	1 (4.3)	1 (4.2)	2 (1.0)	2 (10.5)	1 (5.3)	4 (0.8)
Domestic	93 (16.7)	96 (19.7)	521 (17.5)	5 (21.7)	5 (20.8)	42 (21.4)	4 (21.1)	6 (30.0)	117 (24.6)
Other work	16 (2.9)	10 (2.0)	67 (2.3)	-	1 (4.2)	4 (2.0)	1 (5.3)	1 (5.0)	15 (3.2)
Non-worker	2 (0.4)	3 (0.6)	11 (0.4)	-	1 (4.2)	1 (0.5)	-	-	-
Total	557 (100)	488 (100)	2,972 (100)	23 (100)	24 (100)	196 (100)	19 (100)	20 (100)	476 (100)

Note: Figures in brackets are percentages.

ECONOMIC STATUS

Knowledge about the economic profile of the candidates at all three panchayat levels is important for understanding the distribution of economic power at different levels.

Annual Income Groups

Table 5.9 shows that the economic status of the zilla panchayat executive, in terms of annual income, is better than that of the taluk and gram panchayats.

The direction of increasing economic power is from gram panchayat to zilla panchayat. While nearly 22 per cent of the adhyakshas at the gram and taluk panchayat levels belong to the less than Rs. 5,000 annual income group, none of the zilla panchayat adhyakshas belong to this group. The reverse is true for the high-income groups. Only 1.4 per cent of the adhyakshas at gram panchayat and 8.7 per cent at the taluk panchayat level belong to the more than Rs.1 lakh annual income group, while 26.4 per cent of the adhyakshas at zilla panchayat level belong to this group. This clearly shows the influence of economic factors at all the three levels. This trend is not restricted only to adhyakshas. It can be observed, albeit to a lesser degree, in case of upadhyakshas and members as well.

Asset Distribution

Table 5.10 gives the asset position of panchayat members. The data show that a large majority of the members in all positions own land, with the share of adhyakshas and upadhyakshas being higher. But as far as housing is concerned, no such distinction is observed. About 96 per cent of the members at all positions own a house. Access to modern consumer durables and agricultural implements is higher among the adhyakshas than upadhyakshas and members.

The disaggregated analysis of the adhyakshas and upadhyakshas at various levels (Table 5.11) shows that there is a disparity between the zilla panchayat and the other two levels.

TABLE 5.9
Distribution of Annual Income of Members by Position

Income in Rupees	Gram Panchayat			Taluk Panchayat			Zilla Panchayat		
	A	U	M	A	U	M	A	U	M
< 5,000	124 (22.3)	168 (34.4)	980 (33.0)	5 (21.7)	3 (12.5)	28 (14.3)	-	3 (15.0)	98 (10.1)
5,000 - 10,000	188 (33.8)	148 (30.3)	787 (26.5)	4 (17.4)	7 (29.2)	44 (22.4)	2 (10.5)	6 (30.0)	102 (21.4)
10,001 - 15,000	49 (8.8)	32 (6.6)	270 (9.1)	4 (17.4)	2 (8.3)	31 (15.8)	1 (5.3)	2 (10.0)	37 (7.8)
15,001 - 25,000	88 (15.8)	45 (9.2)	329 (11.1)	3 (13.0)	7 (29.2)	33 (16.8)	-	1 (5.0)	76 (16.0)
25,001 - 50,000	70 (12.6)	48 (9.8)	344 (11.1)	4 (17.4)	4 (16.7)	38 (19.4)	6 (31.6)	3 (15.0)	86 (18.1)
50,001 - 1,00,000	30 (5.4)	36 (7.4)	194 (6.6)	1 (4.3)	1 (4.2)	19 (9.7)	5 (26.4)	2 (10.0)	93 (19.5)
Above 1,00,000	8 (1.4)	11 (2.2)	68 (2.3)	2 (8.7)	-	3 (1.5)	5 (26.4)	3 (15.0)	34 (7.1)

Note: Figures in brackets are percentages.

TABLE 5.10

Ownership of Assets among Members

Assets	Adhyaksha	Upadhyaksha	Member	Total
Land	510 (85.10)	445 (83.6)	2,903 (79.7)	3,858 (80.8)
Livestock	417 (69.6)	346 (65.0)	2,304 (63.2)	3,067 (64.2)
Tractor	54 (9.0)	38 (7.1)	291 (8.0)	383 (8.0)
Tiller	36 (6.0)	17 (3.2)	146 (4.0)	199 (4.2)
Pumpset	231 (38.6)	176 (33.1)	1,200 (32.9)	1,607 (33.7)
Vehicle	210 (35.1)	126 (23.7)	927 (25.4)	1,263 (26.5)
Phone	110 (18.4)	60 (11.3)	477 (13.1)	647 (13.5)
Radio/TV	479 (80.0)	398 (74.8)	2,639 (72.4)	3,516 (73.6)
House	579 (96.7)	519 (97.6)	3,494 (95.9)	4,592 (96.2)
Other assets	156 (26.0)	128 (24.1)	970 (26.6)	1,254 (26.3)

Note: Figures in brackets are percentages.

TABLE 5.11
Distribution of Assets among Members

Assets	Gram Panchayat			Taluk Panchayat			Zilla Panchayat		
	A	U	M	A	U	M	A	U	M
Land	471 (84.6)	406 (83.2)	2,288 (77.0)	23 (100)	21 (87.5)	175 (89.3)	16 (84.2)	18 (90.0)	440 (92.4)
Livestock	386 (69.3)	315 (64.5)	1,822 (52.8)	19 (82.6)	16 (66.7)	130 (66.3)	12 (63.2)	15 (75.0)	352 (73.9)
Tractor	45 (8.1)	31 (6.4)	161 (5.4)	6 (26.1)	3 (12.5)	30 (15.3)	3 (15.8)	4 (20.0)	100 (21.0)
Tiller	29 (5.2)	14 (2.9)	92 (3.1)	- (17.4)	1 (4.2)	13 (6.6)	3 (15.8)	2 (10.0)	41 (8.6)
Pumpset	202 (36.3)	155 (31.8)	840 (28.3)	16 (69.6)	10 (41.7)	85 (43.4)	13 (68.4)	11 (55.0)	275 (57.8)
Vehicles	179 (32.1)	106 (21.7)	584 (19.7)	16 (69.6)	8 (33.3)	91 (46.4)	15 (78.9)	12 (60.0)	252 (52.9)
Phone	84 (15.1)	43 (8.8)	235 (7.9)	9 (39.1)	4 (16.7)	52 (26.5)	17 (89.5)	13 (65.0)	190 (39.9)
Radio/TV	441 (79.2)	356 (73.0)	2,038 (68.6)	21 (91.3)	23 (95.8)	164 (83.7)	17 (89.5)	19 (95.0)	437 (91.8)
House	540 (96.9)	477 (97.7)	2,863 (96.3)	22 (95.7)	23 (95.8)	182 (92.9)	17 (89.5)	19 (95.0)	449 (94.3)
Other	141 (25.3)	115 (23.6)	729 (24.5)	10 (43.5)	6 (25.0)	52 (26.5)	5 (26.3)	7 (35.0)	189 (39.7)

Note: Figures in brackets are percentages.

The asset position of the adhyakshas at the zilla panchayat level is stronger compared to the other two levels, particularly gram panchayat. While 89.5 per cent of the adhyakshas own a telephone at the zilla panchayat level, only 15.1 per cent have such access at the gram panchayat level. The position of the members is not different. While 92 per cent of the members at the zilla level own land, only 77 per cent do so at the gram level. Same is the case with all other assets.

The above analysis shows that the economic position of all the members is comparatively better at the zilla panchayat level than at the other two levels. The adhyakshas and upadhyakshas are better off than the members at all levels.

EXPOSURE TO MASS MEDIA

Exposure to mass media helps in improving the awareness of panchayat members.

TABLE 5.12

Respondents Reading Newspaper/Magazine and Listening to Radio/Watching TV Regularly

Mass Media	Gram Panchayat		Taluk Panchayat		Zilla Panchayat	
	A	U	A	U	A	U
Newspaper/ Magazine	396 (71.1)	309 (63.3)	22 (95.7)	21 (87.5)	18 (94.7)	20 (100)
Radio/TV	452 (81.1)	373 (76.4)	20 (87.0)	21 (87.5)	18 (94.7)	20 (100)

Note: Figures in brackets are percentages.

From the data (Table 5.12) it appears that exposure to the mass media, measured by the habit of reading newspapers/ magazines, listening to radio/watching TV, decreases as one moves down from the zilla panchayat to the gram panchayat level. While nearly 95 per cent of all the candidates read newspapers and listen to the radio regularly at the zilla panchayat level, it is encouraging to note that 81 per cent of the adhyakshas, 76 per cent of the upadhyakshas and 70 per cent of the members listen regularly to the radio or watch TV at the gram panchayat level. The percentages for newspaper reading are lower.

POLITICAL EXPERIENCE

Political Party Affiliations

Most of the respondents reported association with some political party or the other. Table 5.13 shows that most of the adhyakshas and upadhyakshas belong to the JD. Congress (I) is the next preference. BJP and Independents are equally represented among adhyakshas and upadhyakshas.

Party association at the different levels (Table 5.14) shows that while JD is the single strongest party at the zilla panchayat level, the Congress (I) is equally strong at the gram panchayat level. While JD dominates zilla panchayats among the adhyakshas and upadhyakshas, the Congress (I) is strong among the members. But at the gram panchayat it is on the same footing as that of JD among all the members. Thus there is a difference in the political scenario between the gram and taluk panchayat levels on the one hand and the zilla panchayat level on the other. While there is a tendency towards single party domination at the zilla panchayat level, several parties find representation at the gram and taluk panchayat levels.

Ideological Commitment of the Respondents

Social justice appears to be the main ideology of leaders in both positions at all levels. Implementation of Gandhian principles is next importance (Table 5.15). However, in the case of other ideologies, there are differences between the various panchayat levels. There was greater adherence to Dalit ideology at the gram panchayat level. Socialist ideology found no representation among adhyakshas and upadhyakshas at the taluk panchayat level. Sixty-eight adhyakshas at the gram panchayat, three at the taluk panchayat, and two at the zilla panchayat level expressed an indifference towards any given ideology.

TABLE 5.13
Distribution of Panchayat Members by Political Party Affiliations

Party	Adhyakshas	Upadhyakshas	Members
JD	266 (44.4)	243 (45.7)	1,665 (45.7)
Congress(I)	235 (39.2)	206 (38.7)	1,296 (35.6)
BJP	38 (6.3)	28 (5.3)	278 (7.6)
KCP	11 (1.8)	6 (1.1)	69 (1.9)
BSP	-	-	8 (0.2)
CPI	-	1 (0.2)	2 (0.1)
CPI(M)	-	-	7 (0.2)
KRRS	9 (1.5)	7 (1.3)	62 (1.7)
Independent	37 (6.2)	39 (7.3)	226 (6.2)
RPI	-	-	7 (0.2)
VKP	2 (0.3)	-	10 (0.3)
MES	1 (0.2)	2 (0.4)	14 (0.4)

Note: Figures in brackets are percentages.

TABLE 5.14
Political Party Affiliation by Panchayat Level

Party	Gram Panchayat			Taluk Panchayat			Zilla Panchayat		
	A	U	M	A	U	M	A	U	M
Janata Dal	227 (40.8)	205 (42.0)	1,226 (41.3)	21 (91.3)	18 (75.0)	117 (59.7)	18 (94.7)	20 (100)	322 (67.6)
Congress(I)	233 (41.8)	203 (41.6)	1,147 (38.6)	1 (4.3)	3 (12.5)	49 (25.0)	1 (5.3)	-	100 (21.0)
BJP	37 (6.6)	26 (5.3)	223 (7.5)	1 (4.3)	2 (8.3)	22 (11.2)	-	-	33 (6.9)
KCP	11 (2.0)	6 (1.2)	65 (2.2)	-	-	-	-	-	4 (0.8)
Independent	37 (6.6)	39 (8 0)	216 (7.3)	-	-	3 (1.5)	-	-	7 (1.5)
Other	12 (2.2)	9 (1.8)	95 (3.1)	-	1 (4.2)	5 (2.5)	-	-	10 (2.0)

Note: Figures in brackets are percentages.

TABLE 5.15
Distribution of Members by Ideology

Ideology	Gram Panchayat			Taluk Panchayat			Zilla Panchayat		
	A	U	M	A	U	M	A	U	M
Dalit	41 (7.4)	35 (7.2)	265 (8.9)	1 (4.3)	-	14 (7.1)	-	1 (5.0)	18 (3.8)
Social justice	298 (53.5)	268 (54.9)	1,524 (51.3)	14 (60.9)	15 (62.5)	125 (63.8)	12 (63.2)	13 (65.0)	299 (62.8)
Hindutva	18 (3.2)	17 (3.5)	110 (3.7)	1 (4.3)	2 (8.3)	7 (63.6)	-	-	11 (2.3)
Socialist	34 (6.1)	20 (4.1)	155 (5.2)	-	-	13 (6.6)	1 (5.3)	2 (100)	29 (6.1)
Gandhian	67 (12.0)	57 (11.7)	284 (9.6)	4 (17.4)	4 (16.7)	16 (8.2)	2 (10.5)	1 (5.0)	43 (9.0)
Other	3 (0.5)	10 (2.0)	36 (1.2)	-	-	-	-	-	11 (2.3)
No ideology	68 (12.2)	53 (10.9)	417 (14.0)	3 (13.0)	2 (8.3)	15 (7.7)	2 (10.5)	3 (15.0)	47 (9.9)
No information	28 (5.0)	28 (5.7)	181 (6.1)	-	1 (4.2)	-	2 (10.5)	-	18 (3.8)
Total	557 (100)	488 (100)	2,972 (100)	23 (100)	24 (100)	196 (100)	19 (100)	20 (100)	476 (100)

Note: Figures in brackets are percentages.

Participation in Other Associations

Participation of the panchayat members in other associations like cooperatives, youth associations, village sanghas, etc., gives an idea about their activities and social interactions.

Table 5.16 shows that by and large male members participate more actively in other associations than female members.

TABLE 5.16
Members' Participation in Other Associations by Position

Position	Gram Panchayat		Taluk Panchayat		Zilla Panchayat	
	Male	Female	Male	Female	Male	Female
Adhyaksha	205 (65.3)	70 (28.8)	11 (78.6)	5 (55.6)	11 (91.7)	7 (100.0)
Upadhyaksha	142 (53.2)	53 (24.0)	12 (85.7)	5 (50.6)	12 (100.0)	3 (37.5)
Member	970 (54.1)	275 (21.8)	82 (70.1)	24 (30.4)	239 (79.4)	78 (44.6)
Total	1,317 (55.5)	380 (23.1)	105 (72.4)	34 (34.7)	262 (80.6)	88 (46.3)

Note: Figures in brackets are percentages.

Among both male and female members, participation in other associations tended to be higher among adhyakshas. 100 per cent of the female adhyakshas at the zilla panchayat level are members in one or the other association, while only 65.3 per cent of the male adhyakshas and 28.8 per cent of the female adhyakshas at the gram panchayat level are involved with other associations. In case of upadhyakshas 100 per cent participation of males was found at the zilla panchayat level, and while only 37.5 per cent of the females were active at this level.

TABLE 5.17
Association of Other Family Members with Politics

Relationship	Gram Panchayat			Taluk Panchayat			Zilla Panchayat		
	A	U	M	A	U	M	A	U	M
Nobody	435 (75.9)	401 (80.2)	2,521 (83.3)	12 (46.2)	18 (75.0)	148 (71.8)	14 (53.8)	17 (85.0)	318 (60.7)
Father	57 (9.9)	39 (7.8)	209 (6.9)	8 (30.8)	4 (16.7)	26 (12.6)	5 (19.2)	1 (10.0)	89 (17.0)
Mother	7 (1.2)	5 (1.0)	26 (0.9)	-	-	4 (1.9)	1 (3.8)	-	7 (1.3)
Other members (Previous generation)	38 (6.6)	24 (4.8)	121 (4.0)	2 (7.7)	-	12 (5.8)	2 (7.7)	1 (5.0)	45 (8.6)
Brother	10 (1.7)	15 (3.0)	53 (1.8)	1 (3.8)	1 (4.2)	1 (0.5)	2 (7.7)	-	26 (5.0)
Sister	5 (0.9)	-	6 (0.2)	3 (11.5)	1 (4.2)	10 (4.9)	-	-	4 (0.8)
Husband/ Wife	15 (2.6)	11 (2.2)	59 (1.9)	3 (11.5)	1 (4.2)	10 (4.9)	2 (7.7)	-	26 (5.0)
Other members (Present generation)	6 (1.0)	5 (1.0)	32 (1.0)	-	-	5 (2.4)	-	-	9 (1.7)
Total	573 (100)	500 (100)	3,027 (100)	26 (100)	24 (100)	206 (100)	26 (100)	20 (100)	524 (100)

Note: Figures in brackets are percentages.

TABLE 5.18
Priority Issues by Position and Panchayat Level

Priorities	Gram Panchayat			Taluk Panchayat			Zilla Panchayat		
	A	U	M	A	U	M	A	U	M
Education	394 (70.7)	333 (68.2)	1,888 (63.5)	20 (87.0)	21 (87.5)	159 (81.1)	17 (89.4)	19 (95.0)	392 (82.4)
Family planning	49 (8.8)	55 (11.3)	375 (12.6)	1 (4.3)	3 (12.5)	13 (6.6)	-	-	24 (5.0)
Health	63 (11.3)	55 (11.3)	351 (11.8)	2 (8.7)	-	18 (9.2)	-	-	31 (6.5)
Sanitation	28 (5.0)	30 (6.1)	199 (6.7)	-	-	5 (2.6)	1 (5.3)	-	10 (2.1)
Not listed	14 (2.5)	9 (1.8)	66 (2.2)	-	-	1 (0.5)	-	1 (5.0)	12 (2.4)
No priority	9 (1.6)	6 (1.2)	93 (3.1)	-	-	-	1 (5.3)	-	7 (1.6)
Total	557 (100)	488 (100)	2,972 (100)	23 (100)	24 (100)	196 (100)	19 (100)	20 (100)	476 (100)

Note: Figures in brackets are percentages.

Association of Other Family Members with Politics

Table 5.17 gives an idea about the other family members of the elected member who are/were active in politics. There does not appear to be any strong association between the position in the panchayat and relations in politics. However at the taluk level 53.84 per cent and at the zilla level 46.15 per cent of the adhyakshas have their relations in politics. Among them a majority had their fathers in politics – 30.8 per cent at the taluk and 19.2 per cent at the zilla level.

Priorities for the coming Five Years

Education is given first priority by all leaders at all the three tiers. However, the priority accorded to education at the gram panchayat level is lower compared to the other two levels. Family planning, health and sanitation are the other important priorities at the taluk and gram levels. It is to be noted that five per cent of the adhyakshas at the zilla panchayat level did not seem to attach importance to any particular issue. Though female candidates also report education as their first priority, compared to men they give more importance to family planning and health (Table 5.18).

The adhyakshas at the taluk and gram panchayat levels gave priority to health while this was not the case with the zilla panchayat adhyakshas. Only some of the zilla panchayat members mentioned health as a priority.

Chapter VI

Women Representatives

When the panchayati raj system was introduced, very few women contested or got elected. The committees which recommended the creation of panchayati raj institutions (PRIs) did not say much about the role of women in these bodies. The Balwantrai Mehta Committee recommended that in the constitution of panchayats, provisions may be made for the co-option of two women members "who are interested in work among women and children."

The Asoka Mehta Committee had mentioned that two women securing the highest number of votes among the women candidates in the election could take the seats reserved for them, a method of 'co-option by election'. Though PRIs were established in almost all the states, women's representation did not exceed more than two or three. It was only in 1976, after the publication of the Report of the Committee on Status of Women, that there was a demand for the representation of women in panchayati raj bodies through reservation.

Karnataka is a pioneer in this regard. It was the first state in the country to introduce the policy of reservation for women in panchayati raj institutions. Its 1985 Act stipulated that 25 per cent of the total seats should be reserved for women at the district (zilla parishad) and mandal panchayat (a cluster of villages) levels.

Elections to the PRIs according to the 1985 Act were held in 1987. Women occupied 25 per cent of the seats in all the districts. Thus, a large number of women participated in the elections. However, the 1985 Act was superseded by the Karnataka Panchayati Raj Act 1993. This Act incorporated the essential features of the 73rd Constitutional Amendment including reservation of not less than one-third of the total seats for women at all levels. After the 1995 elections, at the GP level alone women occupied 43.3 per cent of the total seats. At the local level they are the political elite.

SOCIO-ECONOMIC PROFILE

An analysis of the socio-economic background of this new leadership is crucial for understanding the kind of women leaders who have emerged in the local government. We interviewed 1,931 women members for the study.

Age

The age distribution of male and female members (Table 6.1) shows that women are entering PRIs at an earlier age than men.

TABLE 6.1
Distribution of Male and Female Members according to Age Groups

Age Group	Gram Panchayat		Taluk Panchayat		Zilla Panchayat	
	Male	Female	Male	Female	Male	Female
Upto 25	8 (3.5)	139 (8.5)	3 (2.1)	27 (27.6)	2 (0.6)	19 (10.0)
26 to 30	322 (13.6)	321 (19.5)	20 (13.8)	19 (19.4)	20 (6.2)	46 (24.2)
31 to 35	427 (18.0)	373 (22.7)	25 (17.2)	25 (25.5)	53 (16.3)	46 (24.2)
36 to 40	556 (23.4)	298 (18.1)	39 (26.9)	14 (14.3)	77 (23.7)	37 (19.5)
41 to 50	683 (28.8)	342 (20.8)	42 (29.0)	10 (10.2)	123 (37.8)	34 (17.9)
51 to 60	221 (9.3)	135 (8.2)	14 (9.7)	3 (3.1)	44 (13.5)	6 (3.2)
Above 60	83 (3.5)	35 (2.1)	1 (0.7)	-	6 (1.8)	2 (1.0)
Total	2,374 (100)	1,643 (100)	145 (100)	98 (100)	325 (100)	190 (100)

Note: Figures in brackets are percentages.

While 17.1 per cent of the male members are below 30 years of age at the gram panchayat level, the share of the female members is 28 per cent. We find a similar trend at the other two levels. At the taluk level the percentages are 15.9 for men and 37.0 for women, and at the zilla level 6.8 males and 34.2 females, respectively. A majority of the male members are above 36 years of age, with the 41 to 50 age group claiming the largest share. This clearly shows that it is the younger generation women who are showing an interest in the PRIs.

Marital Status

The upbringing of girls especially in rural society is oriented towards marriage. It may be seen from the Table 6.2 that a majority of the women members are married (88 per cent). However, single women like widows, divorcees and devadasis have also attained power positions. This is a promising start as it appears that people are not biased, and the significance of marital status as a major determinant of leadership is slowly declining.

TABLE 6.2
Marital Status of Members

Marital Status	Male	Female	Total
Married	2,613 (91.9)	1,699 (88.0)	4,312 (90.3)
Unmarried	212 (7.5)	54 (2.8)	266 (5.6)
Widow/Widower	19 (0.7)	154 (8.0)	173 (3.6)
Divorcee	-	8 (0.4)	8 (0.2)
Devadasi	-	16 (0.8)	16 (0.3)
Total	2,844 (59.6)	1,931 (40.4)	4,775 (100.00)

Note: Figures in brackets are percentages.

TABLE 6.3
Educational Background of Members

Educational Level	Gram Panchayat		Taluk Panchayat		Zilla Panchayat		Overall	
	Male	Female	Male	Female	Male	Female	Male	Female
Illiterate	115 (4.8)	333 (20.3)	3 (2.1)	2 (2.0)	-	6 (3.2)	118 (4.1)	341 (17.7)
Read & write	226 (9.5)	391 (23.8)	3 (2.1)	7 (97.1)	2 (0.6)	9 (4.7)	231 (8.1)	407 (21.1)
Primary	306 (12.9)	261 (15.9)	12 (8.3)	10 (10.2)	5 (1.5)	15 (7.9)	323 (11.4)	286 (14.8)
Higher primary	459 (19.3)	325 (19.8)	23 (15.9)	19 (19.4)	28 (98.6)	30 (15.8)	510 (17.9)	374 (19.4)
Secondary	291 (12.3)	116 (7.1)	15 (10.3)	19 (19.4)	33 (10.2)	32 (16.9)	339 (11.9)	167 (8.6)
SSLC	406 (17.1)	132 (8.0)	27 (18.6)	21 (21.4)	71 (21.8)	36 (18.9)	504 (17.7)	189 (9.8)
PUC	205 (8.6)	42 (2.6)	21 (14.5)	11 (11.2)	47 (14.5)	25 (13.2)	273 (9.6)	78 (4.0)
Graduate	324 (19.0)	33 (2.1)	36 (24.9)	5 (6.1)	119 (36.5)	33 (17.4)	479 (16.9)	72 (3.8)

Table 6.3 Contd...

TABLE 6.3 *Contd.*

Educational Level	Gram Panchayat		Taluk Panchayat		Zilla Panchayat		Overall	
	Male	Female	Male	Female	Male	Female	Male	Female
Postgraduate	14 (0.6)	2 (0.1)	2 (1.4)	3 (3.1)	13 (4.0)	3 (1.6)	29 (1.0)	8 (0.4)
Diploma	22 (0.9)	2 (0.1)	2 (1.4)	-	7 (2.2)	1 (0.5)	31 (1.1)	3 (0.2)
Other	6 (0.3)	6 (0.4)	1 (0.7)	-	-	-	7 (0.2)	6 (0.3)
Total	2,374 (100)	1,643 (100)	145 (100)	98 (100)	325 (100)	190 (100)	2,844 (100)	1,931 (100)

Note: Figures in brackets are percentages.

Educational Background

Table 6.3 shows that illiteracy is higher among women than men. Compared to 4.1 per cent of male members, 17.7 per cent of the female members are illiterate. Illiteracy among female members is higher at the gram panchayat level. However, it is promising to observe that 17.4 per cent of the female members at the zilla panchayat level are graduates.

Caste

Table 6.4 shows the domination of the Backward Classes both among male and female representatives at all levels. However, the extent of domination is lesser in case of female members. There is an equal representation of SCs among male and female members at all levels. Representation of ST women is higher than men within this category.*

TABLE 6.4
Castewise Distribution of Members

Caste	Gram Panchayat		Taluk Panchayat		Zilla Panchayat	
	Male	Female	Male	Female	Male	Female
Forward Caste	111 (4.7)	53 (3.2)	6 (4.2)	7 (7.2)	11 (2.3)	10 (5.3)
Backward Caste	995 (41.8)	579 (35.3)	74 (51.0)	34 (34.6)	168 (51.6)	88 (46.4)
Scheduled Caste	393 (16.5)	266 (16.1)	15 (10.4)	11 (11.2)	35 (10.8)	15 (7.9)
Scheduled Tribe	178 (7.5)	185 (11.2)	11 (7.5)	15 (15.2)	27 (8.2)	25 (13.0)
Other	699 (29.4)	560 (34.1)	39 (26.9)	31 (31.6)	84 (25.9)	52 (27.3)
Total	2,374 (100)	(100)	145 (100)	98 (100)	325 (100)	190 (100)

Note: Figures in brackets are percentage.

* If in a panchayat, only one seat is reserved for STs in total, this lone seat goes to a woman, as there is a constitutional mandate that not less than one-third in each category should be women.

EXPOSURE TO MASS MEDIA

Table 6.5 shows that women members have a lower exposure to mass media compared to men. This is particularly true in the case of newspaper reading at the gram panchayat level. This may be due to the lower literacy rates of rural women.

TABLE 6.5
Members' Exposure to Mass Media

(in percentage)

Mass Media	Gram Panchayat		Taluk Panchayat		Zilla Panchayat	
	Male	Female	Male	Female	Male	Female
Newspaper	79.7	38.0	92.4	80.6	98.8	88.4
Radio/TV	81.0	60.7	90.3	80.6	94.5	89.5

POLITICAL PROFILE

Participation in Association

Participation in other organisations gives members the opportunity for cultivating their talents and enhancing their confidence. Participation of female members in youth associations, mahila mandals, cooperative societies, etc., is very low compared to the male counterparts. Overall, compared to 59.2 per cent of male members, only 26 per cent of female members expressed their association with other organisations (Table 6.6). Disaggregated analysis shows that the participation of female members increases from the gram to the zilla panchayat level. Further, the participation of women is higher among adhyakshas than upadhyakshas.

Previous Political Experience

Table 6.7 shows that lack of previous political experience is higher among female than male members. Only after the introduction of the reservation policy for female candidates,

TABLE 6.6
Participation in Association

Position	Gram Panchayat		Taluk Panchayat		Zilla Panchayat		Overall	
	Male	Female	Male	Female	Male	Female	Male	Female
Adhyaksha	205 (65.3)	70 (28.8)	11 (78.6)	5 (55.6)	11 (91.7)	7 (100)	227 (66.8)	82 (31.7)
Upadhyaksha	142 (53.2)	53 (24.0)	12 (85.7)	5 (50.0)	12 (100)	3 (37.5)	166 (56.7)	61 (25.5)
Members	970 (54.1)	257 (21.8)	82 (70.1)	24 (30.4)	239 (79.4)	78 (44.6)	1,291 (58.4)	359 (25.1)
Total	1,317 (55.5)	380 (23.1)	105 (72.4)	34 (34.7)	262 (80.6)	88 (46.3)	1,684 (59.2)	502 (26.0)

Note: Figures in brackets are percentages to the total of that particular group. For example, in the case of overall, 66.8 per cent of males are participating in any association, indicating that 43.2 per cent of males are not participating.

TABLE 6.7
Previous Political Experience of Members

Position	Gram Panchayat		Taluk Panchayat		Zilla Panchayat		Overall	
	Male	Female	Male	Female	Male	Female	Male	Female
No previous experience	2,012 (84.8)	1,560 (95.0)	90 (62.1)	90 (91.8)	147 (45.2)	161 (84.7)	2,249 (79.1)	1,811 (93.8)
MP	-	-	-	-	1 (0.3)	-	1 (0.04)	-
MLA/MLC	1 (0.04)	-	-	-	1 (0.3)	-	2 (0.1)	-
Mandal/Zilla parishad	272 (11.5)	72 (4.4)	34 (23.5)	7 (7.1)	121 (37.2)	19 (10.0)	427 (15.0)	98 (5.1)
Taluk board	17 (0.7)	2 (0.1)	2 (1.4)	-	29 (8.9)	3 (1.6)	48 (1.7)	5 (0.3)
Other	117 (4.9)	18 (1.1)	27 (18.6)	2 (2.0)	63 (19.4)	8 (4.2)	205 (7.2)	28 (1.5)

Note: Figures in brackets are percentages.

have women started entering PRIs. As against 79.1 per cent males, 94 per cent of the female members do not have any previous political experience. Even among the female candidates there are more freshers at the gram and taluk panchayat levels than at zilla panchayat level. Compared to 95 per cent at the gram panchayat level, 85 per cent women at the zilla panchayat level had some political experience. While a majority of the women with pervious experience worked in mandal/zilla parishads, men had experience both at the parishad and other levels. The "Others" category includes panchayats which existed before the 1983 Act. The respondents referred to them as village and group panchayats.

Motivators

Table 6.8 shows that the motivational forces behind the male and female members are different. Self-motivation due to interest in social service, followed by friends and village community, appear to be the main factors influencing male members. In the case of women, family members, followed by village community and self, appear to be the major motivators. This pattern is observed at all levels. The results show that influence of caste factor in motivating members to enter public life is not substantial.

Ideological Commitment

Table 6.9 shows that social justice is the ideology of the majority of male and female members at all levels. Implementation of Gandhian principles is more important to male members at the gram and taluk panchayat levels compared to the zilla panchayat level. While Hindutva finds more or less an equal number of adherents among men and women at the gram and taluk panchayat levels, at the zilla panchayat level there are almost twice as many male adherents. Even at the zilla panchayat level, where the literacy rate of female members is high, there are more women than men without an ideology.

Though promotion of education is given first priority by a majority of members at all levels, women members in particular preferred family planning and health over education. The reverse was the case with men members.

Table 6.8
Distribution of Panchayat Members by Motivators

Motivators	Gram Panchayat		Taluk Panchayat		Zilla Panchayat		Overall	
	Male	Female	Male	Female	Male	Female	Male	Female
Family members	294 (7.6)	711 (28.2)	18 (8.2)	51 (32.1)	40 (7.4)	106 (33.0)	352 (7.6)	868 (29.0)
Friends	802 (20.8)	301 (12.0)	62 (28.3)	25 (15.7)	124 (22.8)	48 (15.0)	988 (21.4)	374 (12.5)
Zamindar	110 (2.9)	75 (3.0)	3 (1.4)	2 (1.3)	10 (1.8)	6 (1.9)	123 (2.7)	83 (2.8)
Landlord	617 (16.0)	427 (17.0)	24 (11.0)	16 (10.1)	59 (10.8)	38 (11.8)	700 (15.2)	481 (16.0)
Professional organisation	16 (0.4)	5 (0.2)	3 (1.4)	1 (10.6)	3 (0.6)	1 (0.3)	22 (0.5)	7 (0.2)
Self	1,186 (30.7)	354 (14.0)	74 (33.8)	31 (19.5)	193 (35.5)	57 (17.8)	1,453 (31.5)	442 (14.7)
Caste/ Religion	122 (3.2)	67 (2.7)	5 (2.3)	1 (0.6)	16 (2.9)	5 (1.6)	143 (3.1)	73 (2.4)
Village community	637 (16.5)	531 (21.1)	25 (11.4)	31 (19.5)	85 (15.6)	51 (15.9)	747 (16.2)	613 (20.5)
Other	72 (1.9)	46 (1.8)	5 (2.3)	1 (0.6)	14 (2.6)	9 (12.8)	91 (2.0)	56 (1.9)
Total	3,856 (100)	2,517 (100)	219 (100)	159 (100)	544 (100)	321 (100)	4,619 (100)	2,997 (100)

Note: Figures in brackets are percentages.

TABLE 6.9
Distribution of Panchayat Members by Ideology
(in percentage)

Ideology	Gram Panchayat		Taluk Panchayat		Zilla Panchayat	
	Male	Female	Male	Female	Male	Female
Social justice	53.9	49.3	60.0	68.4	64.0	61.0
Hindutva	3.8	3.3	4.8	3.1	10.8	5.8
Gandhian	12.0	7.4	11.7	7.1	3.1	4.7
Dalit	9.5	7.5	6.9	5.1	1.8	2.6
Socialist	5.9	4.2	6.9	3.1	5.8	6.8
No ideology	10.8	17.2	8.3	8.2	8.3	13.2
Any other	1.1	1.5	-	-	2.8	1.1
No information	3.0	100	1.4	5.1	3.4	4.7
Total	100	100	100	100	100	100

TABLE 6.10
Distribution of Panchayat Members by Issue Preference

Priority	Gram Panchayat		Taluk Panchayat		Zilla Panchayat	
	Male	Female	Male	Female	Male	Female
Education	1,660 (69.9)	215 (58.1)	124 (85.5)	76 (77.6)	276 (84.9)	152 (80.0)
Family planning	215 (9.1)	264 (16.1)	8 (5.5)	9 (9.2)	7 (2.20)	17 (8.9)
Health	258 (10.9)	211 (12.8)	10 (6.9)	10 (10.2)	16 (4.9)	15 (7.9)
Sanitation	149 (6.3)	108 (6.6)	2 (1.4)	3 (3.1)	8 (2.5)	3 (1.6)
Not listed above	63 (2.7)	26 (1.6)	1 (0.7)	-	11 (3.4)	2 (1.1)
No priority	29 (1.2)	79 (4.8)	-	-	7 (2.2)	1 (5.5)
Total	237 (100)	1,643 (100)	145 (100)	98 (100)	325 (100)	190 (100)

Note: Figures in brackets are percentages.

Political Party Affiliation

Table 6.11 shows that most women members like their male counterparts have party affiliations. Only 6.3 per cent were independents. It is interesting that all the parties have fielded women candidates, with Janata Dal (46 per cent) and Congress (I) (35.7 per cent) having the highest share. It is clear that all the political parties are responding positively to the participation of women in politics, and there is a growing trend towards setting aside seats for women.

WOMEN PRESIDENTS AND VICE-PRESIDENTS

This section provides a profile of the female heads of the panchayats who play a major role as facilitators of change in the process of rural development.

Marital Status

Table 6.12 shows that a majority of the respondents (89 per cent) are married. A small percentage of widows and single, divorced and *devadasi* women are also represented. Of the four devadasi respondents, three were presidents and one vice-president at the gram panchayat level. They, along with divorced women, were not represented at the taluk and zilla panchayat levels.

Caste

Table 6.13 shows that a majority of the respondents belonged to the Vokkaliga and Lingayat communities. Aadi Karnataka and Kurubas were comparatively better represented than other castes and communities.

Income

The income distribution showed that most of the leaders had an annual income of less than Rs.10,000. While at the gram panchayat level most women had an income below Rs. 5000, at the other two tiers their income fell between Rs.5,000 to 10,000 (see Table 6.14).

TABLE 6.11
Distribution of Members by Political Party Affiliation

Party	Male	Female	Total
Janata Dal	1,286 (45.2)	888 (46.0)	2,174 (45.5)
Congress (I)	1,047 (36.8)	690 (35.7)	1,737 (36.4)
BJP	206 (7.2)	138 (7.1)	344 (7.2)
KCP	51 (1.8)	35 (1.8)	86 (1.8)
BSP	5 (0.2)	5 (0.2)	8 (0.2)
CPI	2 (0.1)	1 (0.1)	3 (0.1)
CPI(M)	6 (0.2)	1 (0.1)	7 (0.1)
KRRS	44 (1.5)	34 (1.8)	78 (1.6)
Independent	181 (6.4)	121 (6.3)	302 (6.3)
RPI	4 (0.1)	3 (0.2)	7 (0.1)
Vatal Kannada Paksha	7 (0.2)	5 (0.3)	12 (0.3)
MES	5 (0.2)	12 (0.6)	17 (0.4)
Total	2,844 (59.6)	1,931 (40.4)	4,775 (100)

Note: Figures in brackets are percentages.

TABLE 6.12
Marital Status of Women Adhyakshas/Upadhyakshas in Panchayat

Marital Status	Gram Panchayat		Taluk Panchayat		Zilla Panchayat		All Panchayats		Total
	Adhya-ksha	Upadhya-ksha	Adhya-ksha	Upadhya-ksha	Adhya-ksha	Upadhya-ksha	Adhya-ksha	Upadhya-ksha	
Married	219 (90.1)	195 (88.2)	9 (100.0)	7 (70.0)	7 (100.0)	6 (75.0)	235 (90.7)	208 (87.0)	443 (89.0)
Single	7 (2.9)	4 (1.8)	-	1 (10.0)	-	2 (25.0)	7 (2.7)	7 (2.9)	14 (2.8)
Widow/Widower	14 (5.8)	20 (9.0)	-	2 (20.0)	-	-	14 (5.4)	22 (9.2)	36 (7.2)
Divorcee	-	1 (0.5)	-	-	-	-	-	1 (0.4)	1 (0.2)
Devadasi	3 (1.2)	1 (0.5)	-	-	-	-	3 (1.2)	1 (0.4)	4 (0.8)
Total	243 (52.4)	221 (47.6)	9 (47.4)	10 (52.6)	7 (46.7)	8 (53.3)	259 (52.0)	239 (48.0)	498 (100.0)

Note: Figures in brackets are percentages.

TABLE 6.13
Caste of Women Adhyakshas/Upadhyakshas in Panchayat

Caste	Gram Panchayat		Taluk Panchayat		Zilla Panchayat		All Panchayats		Total
	Adhya-ksha	Upadhya-ksha	Adhya-ksha	Upadhya-ksha	Adhya-ksha	Upadhya-ksha	Adhya-ksha	Upadhya-ksha	
Adi Karnataka (AK)	31 (12.8)	23 (10.4)	-	1 (10.0)	-	1 (12.5)	31 (12.0)	25 (10.5)	56 (11.2)
Adi Dravida (AD)	1 (.4)	2 (.9)	-	-	-	-	1 (.4)	2 (.8)	3 (.6)
Bhovi	4 (1.6)	5 (2.3)	-	-	1 (14.3)	-	5 (1.9)	5 (2.1)	10 (2.0)
Gowda/Vokkaliga	40 (16.5)	32 (14.5)	-	-	1 (14.3)	-	41 (15.8)	35 (15.6)	76 (15.3)
Lingayat	35 (14.4)	33 (14.9)	-	3 (30.0)	1 (14.3)	3 (37.5)	37 (14.3)	37 (15.5)	74 (14.9)
Brahmin	4 (1.6)	7 (3.2)	1 (11.1)	1 (10.0)	-	-	5 (1.9)	7 (2.9)	12 (2.4)
Bunts/Rai/ Shetty	1 (.4)	1 (.5)	1 (11.1)	-	-	-	1 (.4)	1 (.4)	2 (.4)

Table 6.13 Contd...

TABLE 6.13 *Contd.*

Caste	Gram Panchayat		Taluk Panchayat		Zilla Panchayat		All Panchayats		Total
	Adhya-ksha	Upadhya-ksha	Adhya-ksha	Upadhya-ksha	Adhya-ksha	Upadhya-ksha	Adhya-ksha	Upadhya-ksha	
Kodava	1 (.4)	2 (.9)	-	-	-	-	1 (.4)	2 (.8)	3 (.6)
Konkani Nayak	1 (.4)	1 (.5)	-	-	-	-	1 (.4)	1 (.4)	2 (.4)
Reddy	2 (.8)	1 (.5)	-	-	-	-	3 (1.2)	1 (.4)	4 (.8)
Madiwatar	1 (.4)	1 (.5)	1 (11.1)	-	1 (14.3)	-	2 (.8)	1 (.4)	3 (.6)
Banagiga (Setty)	1 (.4)	1 (.5)	-	-	-	-	2 (.8)	1 (.4)	3 (.6)
Kuruba	20 (8.2)	18 (8.1)	1 (11.1)	-	-	1 (12.5)	21 (8.1)	22 (9.2)	43 (8.6)
Lambani/ Soliga	8 (3.3)	3 (1.4)	1 (11.1)	3 (30.0)	1 (14.3)	1 (12.5)	10 (3.9)	5 (2.1)	15 (3.0)
Gonda	-	2 (.9)	1 (11.1)	1 (10.0)	-	-	-	2 (.8)	2 (.4)

Table 6.13 Contd...

TABLE 6.13 *Contd.*

Caste	Gram Panchayat		Taluk Panchayat		Zilla Panchayat		All Panchayats		Total
	Adhya-ksha	Upadhya-ksha	Adhya-ksha	Upadhya-ksha	Adhya-ksha	Upadhya-ksha	Adhya-ksha	Upadhya-ksha	
Maratna	3 (1.2)	5 (2.3)	-	-	-	-	3 (1.2)	5 (2.1)	8 (1.6)
Naik	15 (6.2)	10 (4.5)	-	-	-	-	15 (5.8)	10 (4.2)	25 (5.0)
Other Hindus	67 (27.6)	68 (30.8)	2 (22.2)	1 (10.0)	1 (14.3)	2 (25.0)	70 (27.0)	71 (29.7)	141 (28.3)
Muslim/ Christian	8 (3.3)	6 (2.7)	1 (11.1)	-	1 (14.3)	-	10 (3.9)	6 (2.5)	16 (3.2)
Total	243 (52.4)	221 (47.6)	9 (47.4)	10 (52.6)	7 (46.7)	8 (53.3)	259 (52.0)	239 (48.0)	498 (100.0)

Note: Figures in brackets are percentages.

TABLE 6.14

Annual Income of Women Adhyakshas/Upadhyakshas in Panchayat

Annual Income	Gram Panchayat		Taluk Panchayat		Zilla Panchayat		All Panchayats		Total
	Adhya-ksha	Upadhya-ksha	Adhya-ksha	Upadhya-ksha	Adhya-ksha	Upadhya-ksha	Adhya-ksha	Upadhya-ksha	
Below 5,000	74 (30.5)	86 (38.9)	2 (22.2)	2 (20.0)	-	1 (12.5)	76 (29.3)	89 (37.2)	165 (33.1)
5,000 to 10,000	89 (36.6)	67 (30.3)	3 (33.3)	4 (40.0)	-	3 (37.5)	92 (35.5)	74 (31.0)	166 (33.3)
10,000 to 15,000	18 (7.4)	9 (4.1)	3 (33.3)	-	-	1 (12.5)	21 (8.1)	10 (4.2)	31 (6.2)
15,000 to 25,000	27 (11.1)	22 (10.0)	1 (11.1)	2 (20.0)	-	-	28 (10.8)	24 (10.0)	52 (10.4)
25,000 to 50,000	24 (9.9)	19 (8.6)	-	1 (10.0)	3 (42.9)	1 (12.5)	27 (10.4)	21 (8.8)	48 (9.6)
50,000 to 75,000	7 (2.9)	5 (2.3)	-	-	-	-	7 (2.7)	5 (2.1)	12 (2.4)
75,000 to 1,00,000	2 (.8)	10 (4.5)	-	1 (10.0)	1 (14.3)	1 (12.5)	3 (1.2)	12 (5.0)	15 (3.0)
1 to 2 lakhs	1 (.4)	3 (1.4)	-	-	3 (42.9)	-	4 (1.5)	3 (1.3)	7 (1.4)
Above 2 lakhs	1 (.4)	-	-	-	-	1 (12.5)	1 (.4)	1 (.4)	2 (.4)
Total	243 (52.4)	221 (47.6)	9 (47.4)	10 (52.6)	7 (46.7)	8 (53.3)	259 (52.0)	239 (48.0)	498 (100.0)

Note: Figures in brackets are percentages.

TABLE 6.15
Ownership of Assets among Women Adhyakshas/Upadhyakshas

Assets		Gram Panchayat		Taluk Panchayat		Zilla Panchayat		All Panchayats		Total
		Adhya-ksha	Upadhya-ksha	Adhya-ksha	Upadhya-ksha	Adhya-ksha	Upadhya-ksha	Adhya-ksha	Upadhya-ksha	
Land	Yes	189 (77.8)	166 (75.1)	9 (100.0)	9 (90.0)	6 (85.7)	7 (87.5)	204 (78.8)	182 (76.2)	386 (77.5)
	No	54 (22.2)	55 (24.9)	-	1 (10.0)	1 (14.3)	1 (12.5)	55 (21.2)	57 (23.8)	112 (22.5)
Livestock	Yes	141 (58.0)	132 (59.7)	7 (77.8)	6 (60.0)	4 (57.1)	5 (62.5)	152 (58.7)	143 (59.8)	295 (59.2)
	No	102 (42.0)	89 (40.3)	2 (22.2)	4 (40.0)	3 (42.9)	3 (37.5)	107 (41.3)	96 (40.2)	203 (40.8)
Tractor	Yes	8 (3.3)	8 (3.6)	2 (22.2)	2 (20.0)	1 (14.3)	1 (12.5)	11 (4.2)	11 (4.6)	22 (4.4)
	No	235 (96.7)	213 (96.4)	7 (77.8)	8 (80.0)	6 (85.7)	7 (87.5)	248 (95.8)	228 (95.4)	476 (95.6)
Tiller	Yes	6 (2.5)	5 (2.3)	2 (22.2)	1 (10.0)	2 (28.6)	-	10 (3.9)	6 (2.5)	16 (3.2)
	No	237 (97.5)	216 (97.7)	7 (77.8)	9 (90.0)	5 (71.4)	8 (100.0)	249 (96.1)	233 (97.5)	482 (96.8)

Table 6.15 Contd...

TABLE 6.15 *Contd.*

Assets		Gram Panchayat		Taluk Panchayat		Zilla Panchayat		All Panchayats		Total
		Adhya-ksha	Upadhya-ksha	Adhya-ksha	Upadhya-ksha	Adhya-ksha	Upadhya-ksha	Adhya-ksha	Upadhya-ksha	
Pumpset	Yes	55 (22.6)	53 (24.0)	3 (33.3)	5 (50.0)	5 (71.4)	5 (62.5)	63 (24.3)	63 (26.4)	126 (25.3)
	No	188 (77.4)	168 (76.0)	6 (66.7)	5 (50.0)	2 (28.6)	3 (37.5)	196 (75.7)	176 (73.6)	372 (74.7)
Other agricultural assets	Yes	45 (18.5)	39 (17.6)	2 (22.2)	4 (40.0)	1 (14.3)	3 (37.5)	48 (18.5)	46 (19.2)	94 (18.9)
	No	198 (81.5)	182 (82.4)	7 (77.8)	6 (60.0)	6 (85.7)	5 (62.5)	211 (81.5)	193 (80.8)	404 (81.1)
Vehicle	Yes	45 (18.5)	37 (16.7)	6 (66.7)	3 (30.0)	5 (71.4)	5 (62.5)	56 (21.6)	45 (18.8)	101 (20.3)
	No	198 (81.5)	184 (83.3)	3 (33.3)	7 (70.0)	2 (28.6)	3 (37.5)	203 (78.4)	194 (81.2)	397 (79.7)
Phone	Yes	15 (6.2)	15 (6.8)	3 (33.3)	1 (10.0)	7 (100.0)	5 (62.5)	25 (9.7)	21 (8.8)	46 (9.2)
	No	228 (93.8)	206 (93.2)	6 (66.7)	9 (90.0)	-	3 (37.5)	234 (90.3)	218 (91.2)	452 (90.8)

Table 6.15 Contd...

TABLE 6.15 *Contd.*

Assets		Gram Panchayat		Taluk Panchayat		Zilla Panchayat		All Panchayats		Total
		Adhya-ksha	Upadhya-ksha	Adhya-ksha	Upadhya-ksha	Adhya-ksha	Upadhya-ksha	Adhya-ksha	Upadhya-ksha	
Radio/TV	Yes	181 (74.5)	155 (70.1)	7 (77.8)	9 (90.0)	7 (100.0)	7 (87.5)	195 (75.3)	171 (71.5)	366 (73.5)
	No	62 (25.5)	66 (29.9)	2 (22.2)	1 (10.0)	-	1 (12.5)	64 (24.7)	68 (28.5)	132 (26.5)
House	Own	232 (95.5)	213 (96.4)	9 (100.0)	9 (90.0)	6 (85.7)	7 (87.5)	247 (95.4)	229 (95.8)	476 (95.6)
	Rented	11 (4.5)	8 (3.6)	-	1 (10.0)	1 (14.3)	1 (12.5)	12 (4.6)	10 (4.2)	22 (4.4)

Note: Figures in brackets are percentages.

TABLE 6.16
Occupation of Women Adhyakshas/Upadhyakshas in Panchayat

Occupation	Gram Panchayat		Taluk Panchayat		Zilla Panchayat		All Panchayats		Total
	Adhya-ksha	Upadhya-ksha	Adhya-ksha	Upadhya-ksha	Adhya-ksha	Upadhya-ksha	Adhya-ksha	Upadhya-ksha	
Agriculture	122 (50.2)	93 (42.1)	4 (44.4)	3 (30.0)	3 (42.9)	2 (25.0)	129 (49.8)	98 (41.0)	227 (45.6)
Craftsmen	2 (.8)	1 (.5)	-	-	-	-	2 (.8)	1 (.4)	3 (.6)
Self-employment	12 (4.9)	8 (3.6)	1 (11.1)	1 (10.0)	-	-	13 (5.0)	9 (3.8)	22 (4.4)
Domestic work	89 (36.6)	95 (43.0)	4 (44.4)	5 (50.0)	4 (57.1)	6 (75.0)	97 (37.5)	106 (44.4)	203 (40.8)
Petty trader	3 (1.2)	2 (.9)	-	-	-	-	3 (1.2)	2 (.8)	5 (1.0)
Teacher/ Lecturer	1 (.4)	-	-	-	-	-	1 (.4)	-	1 (.2)
Agricultural labour	11 (4.5)	20 (9.0)	-	-	-	-	11 (4.2)	20 (8.4)	31 (6.2)
Other	3 (1.2)	2 (.9)	-	-	-	-	3 (1.2)	2 (.8)	5 (1.0)
Non-worker	-	-	-	1 (10.0)	-	-	-	1 (.4)	1 (.2)
Total	243 (52.4)	221 (47.6)	9 (47.4)	10 (52.6)	7 (46.7)	8 (53.3)	259 (52.0)	239 (48.0)	498 (100.0)

Note: Figures in brackets are percentages.

TABLE 6.17
Political Party Affiliation of Women Adhyakshas/Upadhyakshas in Panchayat

Party	Gram Panchayat		Taluk Panchayat		Zilla Panchayat		All Panchayats		Total
	Adhya-ksha	Upadhya-ksha	Adhya-ksha	Upadhya-ksha	Adhya-ksha	Upadhya-ksha	Adhya-ksha	Upadhya-ksha	
Janata Dal	101 (41.6)	88 (39.8)	8 (88.9)	9 (90.0)	6 (85.7)	8 (100.0)	115 (44.4)	105 (43.9)	220 (44.2)
Congress(I)	93 (38.3)	93 (42.1)	1 (11.1)	-	1 (14.3)	-	95 (36.7)	93 (38.9)	188 (37.8)
BJP	17 (7.0)	20 (9.0)	-	1 (10.0)	-	-	17 (6.6)	21 (8.8)	38 (7.6)
KCP	4 (1.6)	1 (.5)	-	-	-	-	4 (1.5)	1 (.4)	5 (1.0)
CPI	-	1 (.5)	-	-	-	-	-	1 (.4)	1 (.2)
KRRS	6 (2.5)	3 (1.4)	-	-	-	-	6 (2.3)	3 (1.3)	9 (1.8)
Independent	20 (8.2)	13 (5.9)	-	-	-	-	20 (7.7)	13 (5.4)	33 (6.6)
Vatal Kannada Paksha	2 (.8)	-	-	-	-	-	2 (.8)	-	2 (.4)
MES	-	2 (.9)	-	-	-	-	-	2 (.8)	2 (.4)
Total	243 (52.4)	221 (47.6)	9 (47.4)	10 (52.6)	7 (46.7)	8 (53.3)	259 (52.0)	239 (48.0)	498 (100.0)

Note: Figures in brackets are percentages.

Table 6.18
Ideological Commitment of Women Adhyakshas/Upadhyakshas in Panchayat

Ideology	Gram Panchayat		Taluk Panchayat		Zilla Panchayat		All Panchayats		Total
	Adhya-ksha	Upadhya-ksha	Adhya-ksha	Upadhya-ksha	Adhya-ksha	Upadhya-ksha	Adhya-ksha	Upadhya-ksha	
Dalit	19 (7.8)	10 (4.5)	1 (11.1)	-	-	-	20 (7.7)	10 (4.2)	30 (6.0)
Social justice	131 (53.9)	114 (51.6)	4 (44.4)	6 (60.0)	4 (57.1)	5 (62.5)	139 (53.7)	125 (52.3)	264 (53.0)
Hindutva	7 (2.9)	11 (5.0)	-	-	-	-	7 (2.7)	12 (5.0)	19 (3.8)
Socialistic	12 (4.9)	5 (2.3)	-	1 (10.0)	-	-	12 (4.6)	5 (2.1)	17 (3.4)
Gandhian	20 (8.2)	23 (10.4)	3 (33.3)	1 (10.0)	1 (14.3)	-	24 (9.3)	24 (10.0)	48 (9.6)
Any other	2 (.8)	5 (2.3)	-	-	-	-	2 (.8)	5 (2.1)	7 (1.4)
No ideology	32 (13.2)	23 (12.7)	1 (11.1)	1 (10.0)	1 (14.3)	3 (37.5)	34 (13.1)	32 (13.4)	66 (13.3)
No information/ Do not know	20 (8.2)	25 (11.3)	-	1 (10.0)	1 (14.3)	-	21 (8.1)	26 (10.9)	47 (9.4)
Total	243 (52.4)	221 (47.6)	9 (47.4)	10 (52.6)	7 (46.7)	8 (53.3)	259 (52.0)	239 (48.0)	498 (100.0)

Note: Figures in brackets are percentages.

Table 6.19
Reading Habits of Women Adhyakshas/Upadhyakshas in Panchayat

Reading News-papers	Gram Panchayat		Taluk Panchayat		Zilla Panchayat		All Panchayats	
	Adhya-ksha	Upadhya-ksha	Adhya-ksha	Upadhya-ksha	Adhya-ksha	Upadhya-ksha	Adhya-ksha	Upadhya-ksha
Yes	117 (48.1)	91 (41.2)	8 (88.9)	8 (80.0)	6 (85.7)	8 (100.0)	131 (50.6)	107 (44.8)
No	126 (51.9)	130 (58.8)	1 (11.1)	2 (20.0)	1 (14.3)	-	128 (49.4)	132 (55.2)
Total	243 (52.4)	221 (47.6)	9 (47.4)	10 (52.6)	7 (46.7)	8 (53.3)	259 (52.0)	239 (48.0)

Note: Figures in brackets are percentages.

Table 6.20
Listening to Radio/WatchingTV among Women Adhyakshas/Upadhyakshas in Panchayat

Listening to/watch-ing radio/TV	Gram Panchayat		Taluk Panchayat		Zilla Panchayat		All Panchayats	
	Adhya-ksha	Upadhya-ksha	Adhya-ksha	Upadhya-ksha	Adhya-ksha	Upadhya-ksha	Adhya-ksha	Upadhya-ksha
Yes	174 (71.6)	147 (66.5)	6 (66.7)	8 (80.0)	6 (85.7)	8 (100.0)	186 (71.8)	163 (68.2)
No	69 (28.4)	74 (33.5)	3 (33.3)	2 (20.0)	1 (14.3)	-	73 (28.2)	76 (31.8)
Total	243 (52.4)	221 (47.6)	9 (47.4)	10 (52.6)	7 (46.7)	8 (53.3)	259 (52.0)	239 (48.0)

Ownership of Assets

Most of the women presidents and vice-presidents owned land and livestock. Some of them owned pumpset and other agricultural assets. The percentages were higher at the taluk and zilla levels. A number of women also possessed radios and television sets, and sometimes even a vehicle and a telephone (Table 6.15).

Occupation

Table 6.16 shows that overall agriculture is the main occupation of women panchayat leaders. This is closely followed by domestic work, which in fact has a higher share than agriculture at the zilla panchayat level. A few of the respondents are self-employed. Almost half of the women respondents do not have a second occupation and nearly half mentioned domestic work as their second occupation.

Political Party Affiliation

Table 6.17 shows that Janata Dal has the maximum number of women presidents and vice-presidents, followed by Congress (I). BJP has some presence. KCP, CPI and KRRS have negligible representation. A small percentage (6.6 per cent) of women are Independents.

Commitment to Ideology

Table 6.18 shows that a majority of women representatives mentioned social justice as their main ideology. About 53 per cent of the women presidents and vice-presidents are committed to social justice. Adherence to ideologies like Gandhian, Dalit, socialist and Hindutva is considerably less.

Exposure to Mass Media

Tables 6.19 and 6.20 show that 50.6 per cent of the women presidents and 44.8 per cent of the vice-presidents read newspapers; a greater percentage watch television and listen to radio, i.e., 71.8 per cent of presidents and 68.2 per cent vice-presidents.

Chapter VII

Major Findings and Reflections

The second part of the present study was to understand the socio-economic background of the members of the PRIs in Karnataka. The following dimensions were studied.

Panchayat Members

In terms of age, it was found that young and middle-aged people are emerging in leadership positions at the grassroot level. It appears that older people are withdrawing from leadership roles with the passage of time. Most of the respondents were married. Out of 4,775 members, 16 had been devadasis. They managed to get elected to the gram panchayat only. Women belonging to this community are generally looked down by society. Yet, this did not act as a taboo on the emerging leadership. It is very encouraging and indicative of positive social change.

Regarding family structure, namely joint or nuclear, the data suggest that even now the joint family is a salient feature of the rural social fabric. This is reflective of the traditions of an agricultural society where family status dominates over individual standing.

Data on the number of children is interesting. It shows that a majority of the members have three to four children. People are thus going in for medium-sized families. It is an indication of the health and family welfare activities in the state.

The landholding capacity generally differentiates the rich farmer from the poor cultivator and determines the economic status of an individual in the village. It was found that a majority of the members own land at the two higher tiers, while at the gram panchayat level there are more landless. The share of members with irrigated land is also higher at the taluk and zilla panchayat levels compared to the gram panchayat level.

The data on economic background thus show that the zilla panchayat level is dominated by the rich landowning class depending mainly on agriculture for its livelihood. At the gram panchayat level, a majority of the members belong to landless, low-income groups which depend on wage labour. The taluk panchayat members fall between these two extremes, tending more towards the characteristics of the zilla panchayat members.

Though agriculture is the main occupation of most of the respondents, leaders are also engaged in other economic activities like crafts, self-employment, petty business, etc.

Exposure to mass media in terms of reading newspapers, listening to radio, and watching television is common at all levels, though it shows a decreasing trend from the zilla to the gram panchayat level.

Data related to level of education reveal that even now illiteracy prevails and a small percentage of illiterates have become members. But, it is encouraging to note that educated persons, some highly qualified, are entering public life and occupying leadership positions.

It is important that leaders in an organisation be committed to social development. They should be aware of the realities around them. The study shows that most respondents expressed the need to improve the existing conditions in rural areas. For this they mentioned extension and improvement of educational facilities as their first priority. The need for improving health status, family planning, and sanitation also was duly recognised.

A common belief is that experience in politics and public life enhances a leader's maturity and equips him or her for leadership positions and consequently such leaders are preferred. But the findings of this study do not show any such relation between political experience and leadership patterns. In fact this category of seasoned politicians is disappearing and a new class of leaders has emerged.

Leadership still revolves around two major political parties – Janata Dal and Congress (I). However, other political parties are gradually entering local bodies. The number of independent contestants is meagre and the orientation towards left parties such as CPI and CPI(M) is negligible.

The parties' interest in panchayats may be attributed to the considerable powers the panchayats have acquired over the years. The parties are well aware of the importance of these bodies and the influence that a panchayat president wields in the village as a key political figure. The political parties thus have a vested interest in controlling local bodies.

With reservations for SC/ST women and BCs under the 1993 Act, major changes have occurred since its implementation. The percentage of Vokkaligas and Lingayats, the two dominant castes in the overall leadership and which hitherto dominated grassroots institutions, in local bodies has considerably declined. At the gram panchayat level even devadasis have become members. This can be considered as a major step forward in tackling and eradicating the abhorrent devadasi system. Religious minorities have some representation. Likewise, leadership has shifted to the less privileged sections of society as inferred from the annual income patterns.

Adhyakshas and Upadhyakshas

The trend from our sample (4,775 elected representatives) shows the domination of Backward Classes in the adhyakshas and upadhyakshas posts. The representation of SCs is lower among adhyakshas compared to upadhyakshas and members. BC domination is higher among the adhyakshas at the taluk and zilla panchayat levels. Conversely, SC representation is higher among adhyakshas at the gram panchayat level.

With regard to ownership of assets, a majority of the adhyakshas and upadhyakshas own land. Their access to modern consumer durables and agricultural implements is also higher compared to members.

Primary and secondary occupational analyses show that cultivation is the main occupation for a majority of adhyakshas. For women, domestic work is the next major occupation. Agricultural labour is one of the main occupations among adhyakshas at the gram panchayat level. This is absent among the adhyakshas at the taluk and zilla panchayat levels.

Most of the respondents are affiliated to a political party. The maximum number of Adhyakshas and Upadhyakshas belong to Janata Dal; Congress (I) has the next largest share. BJP and independents are equally strong. Janata Dal is the single strongest party at the zilla panchayat level. Congress (I) is equally strong at the gram panchayat level. There is single party domination at the zilla level, whereas there is some amount of diversification at the gram panchayat level.

Social justice is the ideology of a majority of adhyakshas and upadhyakshas at all levels. Gandhian principles and justice for Dalits were other important ideologies.

A large percentage of the adhyakshas and upadhyakshas are members of a variety of socio-cultural associations and cooperatives. The data reveal a higher participation by male leaders in other associations than female leaders.

Education is given the first priority by a majority of the adhyakshas and upadhyakshas at all three levels. Family planning, health and sanitation are the other important priorities. It was observed that though there is higher illiteracy at the gram panchayat level, a lower percentage at this tier accords education first priority. Health is given higher priority at the taluk and zilla panchayat levels.

There is an increase in the economic power of leaders as we proceed from the gram to the zilla panchayat level. The zilla panchayat adhyakshas belong to high-income groups and those of gram panchayat to low-income groups. Taluk adhyakshas fall in between. The same is the case with upadhyakshas but to a lesser degree.

A majority of the adhyakshas and upadhyakshas are literate. In some cases graduates and postgraduates have taken up leadership positions.

Women Members

Most of the women members are younger than their male counterparts, are married, and have children. Their family members, especially the husbands, had been or are engaged in political activities.

Most of the women members are not economically well-off, especially at the gram panchayat level. Though a majority of them belong to the dominant castes, other sections of the society are also represented. Hence the importance of caste as a factor influencing leadership is declining.

It is seen that widows, devadasis and single women are also represented to some degree.

Illiteracy is higher among women than men members and is more glaring at the gram panchayat level. However, there are female graduates in the PRIs especially at the zilla panchayat level. Low literacy has a direct impact on newspaper reading and TV watching habits; exposure to such mass media is much lower among women members. Also, women are not active participants in other organisations or associations.

Illiteracy among female adhyakshas and upadhyakshas is also considerably higher, particularly at the gram panchayat level. However, the percentage of graduates among female leaders is higher at the zilla panchayat level.

Another finding was that family members or the husband in many cases have motivated the women to contest. Self-motivation to contest local elections is lower among women, especially at the gram panchayat level.

Women members appear to be aware of the social reality around them. They stressed social justice and education as their main ideology and priority. Family planning and health were also considered important by women members.

All the political party organisations are mobilising women to join politics. In this study most of the women are members of political parties. The Janata Dal has the maximum number of women members followed by the Congress (I).

An examination of the socio-economic background of the different categories of members of the PRIs reveal that most of them are young or middle-aged, economically less privileged, have membership in political parties, are educated, and represent various castes. The study found that the present system has largely new entrants. Many of the leaders are the first in their families to enter politics. For the first time a large number of women have become members, presidents and vice-presidents. Now that women and the other weaker sections have gained entry into panchayats, political education is needed to ensure their effective participation. In addition to educating them about the relevance of the panchayati raj system, and the rights, responsibilities and functions of the committees, they should be made aware of the current political developments, policies and schemes for their upliftment. A mechanism should be instituted for making such information accessible. Training and orientation should be the first step towards building awareness among the hitherto politically inexperienced strata of society.

The gram sabha is a pivotal body for the articulation of the felt needs of the people. It has provided an opportunity for people to participate in the process of rural development. Its proper functioning is thus of utmost importance for the success of the panchayati raj system. Through the gram sabha, rural masses can be effectively brought into the planning, decision-making, monitoring and implementation processes.

It was found that even the educated lacked an understanding of the panchayati raj system and its functioning, especially of the committees. This is discouraging. Therefore, immediately after the elections, all members should undergo an orientation programme on the panchayati raj system, followed by periodic training or refresher courses to update their understanding of the functioning of the system. This will require well-trained resource persons or experts because the success of the programme will depend on the extent of the trainer's knowledge and commitment. Inclusion of women experts is important as they better understand the fears, strengths and aspirations of their fellow women.

It has been generally observed that political parties create friction among people. Panchayats are more effective if they function on the basis of consensus. The vote should therefore not be used to pit members against one another. Political parties working at the grassroots level have a major responsibility of facilitating effective functioning of panchayati bodies through the politics of consensus.

Non-government organisations, which have emerged as the most important forum for the organised articulation of problems and issues of people, can play a crucial role in creating well-informed public opinion. They can also train leaders to exercise effective local control and thereby ensure meaningful political participation. Organisations already working in different areas can step in until fullfledged resource centres come up. Existing voluntary organisations can be developed into information centres and act as forums for information dissemination, discussions, networking, and data bank services.

Academic and research organisations and the government should be equal partners in taking up the responsibility of creating politically conscious citizens capable of bringing about positive social change.

Reservations play a crucial role in breaking the stranglehold of traditionally dominant sections on PRIs. Leadership is no longer confined to a particular class, caste or gender. This reflects the strength of our democratic structures and political processes. The system has given scope for the vulnerable sections of society to enter politics, and has seen the emergence of a new leadership, determined by the 'achieved status' of an individual.

If the objective of local representative governments is to play a more effective role in the political process of society, constant efforts will have to be made to strengthen them in the direction of decentralisation of powers and functions. This will afford greater opportunities for people's involvement in the management of local affairs. PRIs should be viewed as training grounds for future statesmen and politicians, and as the arena of political education of citizens in general.

Panchayati raj institutions are the most important channels for popular participation in the development process. As they deal with the day-to-day affairs of the rural masses, they should have close links with the people and continue to draw up ways and means to serve them. Decentralisation and wholesome people's participation for which these institutions have already laid the foundation will go a long way in bridging the existing class, caste and gender disparities. This is a promising start for a just and egalitarian society.

REFERENCES

Amal Ray and Jayalaksmi Kumpatla, 'Zilla Parishad Presidents in Karnataka: Their Social Background and Implications for Development', *Economic and Political Weekly*, vol. XXII, nos. 42 and 43, 17-24 Oct 1987.

Anand Inbanathan, 'The New Panchayati Raj System in Karnataka: An Evaluation', ISS Manuscript Report Series, New Delhi, 1992.

Bhargava B S, C R Bada and Vijay N Torgal, *Panchayati Raj System in Karnataka*, Jackson Publications, New Delhi, 1982.

Bhargava B S and Shivanna, 'Emerging Pattern of Leadership in Panchayati Raj System: Caste Study of a Zilla Parishad in Karnataka', Working Paper, Institute for Social and Economic Change, Bangalore, 1990.

Bhargava B S and Subha K, 'Political Empowerment of Women. The Case of Karnataka's Experience with Panchayati Raj', *Political Economy Journal of India*, nos. 3 & 4, July-Dec 1994.

George Mathew, ed., *Panchayati Raj in Karnataka Today: Its National Dimensions*, Concept Publishing Company, New Delhi, 1986.

George Mathew, *Panchayati Raj: From Legislation to Movement*, Concept Publishing Company, New Delhi, 1994.

Government of Karnataka, The Karnataka Panchayati Raj Act 1993, Government Press, Bangalore.

Government of Karnataka, The Karnataka Zilla Parishads, Taluk Panchayat Samithis, Mandal Panchayats and Nyaya Panchayats Act 1985, Government Press, Bangalore.

Government of Karnataka, *Karnataka State Gazetteer II*, Karnataka Gazetteer Department, 1983.

Institute of Social Sciences, 'Social Background of Zilla Parishad Members in Karnataka, 1989,' ISS Occasional Paper Series 6, New Delhi, 1989.

Institute of Social Sciences, 'Karnataka Mandal Panchayat Members' Social Background, 1990,' ISS Occasional Paper Series 7, New Delhi, 1990.

Institute of Social Sciences, 'Karnataka Jilla Parishad Mattu Mandala Panchayati Sadasyara Samajika Hinnale 1990,' (in Kannada), 1991.

Subha K, 'Training: An Aid to Empower Rural Women Leaders', *Kurukshetra*, April 1995.

Appendices

APPENDIX I

District Panchayats: Basic Data

Sl. No.	Name of the District	No. of Gram Pancha-yats	No. of Mandal Pancha-yats	Total seats	No. of seats reserved for women	Total Rural population
1.	Bangalore (U)	115	-	1,713	626	6,69,909
2.	Bangalore (R)	226	102*	3,533	1,527	13,69,908
3.	Chitradurga	275	116	4,159	1,731	15,91,765
4.	Kolar	305	125	4,385	1,951	16,99,906
5.	Shimoga	364	165	3,565	1,739	14,03,421
6.	Tumkur	320	145	4,931	2,093	19,23,656
7.	Chickmagalur	225	107	2,203	1,087	8,45,422
8.	Dakshina Kannada	354	167	5,182	2,260	19,31,670
9.	Hassan	256	104	3,422	1,536	12,96,962
10.	Kodagu	96	60	1,091	509	4,10,514
11.	Mandya	228	99	3,556	1,505	13,77,570
12.	Mysore	361	160	5,891	2,499	22,24,724
13.	Belgaum	473	202	7,206	3,147	27,41,820
14.	Bijapur	363	164	5,677	2,456	22,39,244
15.	Dharwad	439	163	5,832	2,562	22,79,259
16.	Uttara Kannada	209	125	2,402	1,135	9,25,744
17.	Bellary	220	89	3,374	1,435	13,25,692
18.	Bidar	176	73	2,629	1,124	10,10,096
19.	Gulbarga	336	166	5,095	2,256	19,72,366
20.	Raichur	299	139	4,781	2,002	18,29,765
	Total	5,640	2,471	80,627	35,180	

* Nelamangla Town Municipality was converted into a Mandal Panchayat taking the number of Mandal Panchayats to 103 after the 1987 elections.

Source: Karnataka Election Commission.

APPENDIX II

Reservation of Seats in Gram Panchayats

Sl. No.	Name of District	No. of Gram Panchayats	Total Seats	Seats Reserved			
				SC	ST	BC	General
1.	Bangalore (U)	115	1,713	457	121	570	565
2.	Bangalore (R)	226	3,533	767	249	1,183	1,334
3.	Chitradurga	275	4,159	974	734	1,361	1,090
4.	Kolar	305	4,385	1,175	456	1,447	1,307
5.	Shimoga	364	3,565	940	409	1,187	1,029
6.	Tumkur	320	4,931	1,076	482	1,642	1,731
7.	Chickmagalur	225	2,203	548	234	729	692
8.	Dakshina Kannada	354	5,182	950	426	1,719	2,087
9.	Hassan	256	3,422	785	260	1,144	1,233
10.	Kodagu	96	1,091	216	137	368	370
11.	Mandya	228	3,556	684	228	1,188	1,456
12.	Mysore	361	5,891	1,412	459	1,966	2,054
13.	Belgaum	473	7,206	1,279	548	2,393	2,986
14.	Bijapur	363	5,677	1,241	380	1,893	2,163
15.	Dharwad	439	5,832	1,176	492	1,947	2,217
16.	Uttara Kannada	209	2,402	480	218	802	902
17.	Bellary	220	3,374	794	435	1,111	1,034
18.	Bidar	176	2,629	633	323	882	791
19.	Gulbarga	336	5,095	1,343	442	1,706	1,604
20.	Raichur	299	4,781	988	542	1,590	1,661
	Total	5,640	80,627	17,906	7,575	26,828	28,306

Source: Karnataka Election Commission.

APPENDIX III
Reservation of Seats in Taluk Panchayats

Sl. No.	Name of District	No. of Seats	SC	ST	OBC 80%	OBC 20%	Other
1.	Bangalore (U)	69 (27)	18 (7)	1 (1)	19 (8)	4 (1)	27 (10)
2.	Bangalore (R)	143 (27)	30 (12)	5 (5)	38 (15)	9 (2)	61 (23)
3.	Chitradurga	172 (70)	38 (15)	30 (13)	46 (20)	12 (3)	46 (19)
4.	Kolar	186 (80)	49 (21)	17 (11)	51 (25)	11 -	58 (23)
5.	Shimoga	148 (62)	28 (14)	6 (4)	40 (19)	10 (1)	64 (24)
6.	Tumkur	203 (80)	38 (15)	17 (9)	54 (22)	14 (4)	80 (30)
7.	Chickmagalur	105 (46)	21 (10)	2 (2)	29 (15)	7 (1)	46 (18)
8.	D. Kannada	206 (82)	15 (8)	9 (7)	54 (22)	14 (5)	114 (40)
9.	Hassan	143 (56)	26 (11)	-	37 (16)	11 (3)	69 (26)
10.	Kodagu	48 (19)	7 (3)	5 (3)	13 (6)	3 -	20 (7)
11.	Mandya	147 (56)	22 (10)	-	38 (14)	11 (4)	76 (28)
12.	Mysore	243 (94)	52 (20)	8 (6)	65 (25)	16 (5)	102 (38)
13.	Belgaum	287 (107)	32 (14)	6 (4)	75 (26)	19 (8)	155 (55)
14.	Bijapur	226 (84)	42 (16)	2 (2)	61 (24)	15 (4)	106 (38)
15.	Dharwad	248 (106)	31 (17)	7 (6)	67 (36)	17 -	126 (47)
16.	U. Kannada	123 (57)	11 (10)	1 (1)	33 (22)	11 -	67 (24)
17.	Bellary	137 (55)	30 (12)	15 (7)	37 (18)	9 (1)	46 (17)
18.	Bidar	107 (43)	24 (10)	10 (5)	30 (14)	6 (1)	37 (13)
19.	Gulbarga	204 (81)	52 (20)	10 (7)	55 (24)	12 (2)	75 (28)
20.	Raichur	195 (81)	35 (16)	18 (11)	52 (18)	12 (7)	78 (29)
	Total	3,340 (1,343)	601 (261)	169 (104)	894 (389)	223 (52)	1,453 (537)

Note: Figures in brackets indicate seats reserved for women.

APPENDIX IV
Reservation of Seats in Zilla Panchayats

Sl. No.	Name of District	No. of Seats	SC	ST	OBC		Other
					80%	20%	
1.	Bangalore (U)	18 (7)	5 (2)	-	5 (2)	1 -	7 (3)
2.	Bangalore (R)	38 (15)	8 (3)	1 (1)	10 (4)	3 (1)	16 (6)
3.	Chitradurga	46 (17)	10 (5)	8 (3)	12 (4)	3 (1)	13 (5)
4.	Kolar	50 (19)	13 (5)	4 (2)	14 (5)	3 (1)	16 (6)
5.	Shimoga	41 (15)	8 (3)	2 (1)	11 (4)	3 (1)	17 (6)
6.	Tumkur	54 (20)	10 (4)	4 (2)	14 (5)	4 (1)	22 (8)
7.	Chickmagalur	33 (13)	7 (3)	1 (1)	9 (4)	2 -	14 (5)
8.	D. Kannada	55 (19)	4 (2)	3 (1)	14 (5)	4 (1)	30 (10)
9.	Hassan	37 (13)	7 (3)	-	10 (3)	2 (1)	18 (6)
10.	Kodagu	27 (10)	3 (1)	2 (1)	7 (3)	2 -	13 (5)
11.	Mandya	39 (14)	5 (2)	-	10 (4)	3 (1)	21 (7)
12.	Mysore	64 (22)	14 (5)	2 (1)	17 (6)	4 (1)	27 (9)
13.	Belgaum	76 (27)	9 (3)	2 (1)	20 (7)	5 (2)	40 (14)
14.	Bijapur	60 (22)	11 (4)	1 (1)	16 (6)	4 (1)	28 (10)
15.	Dharwad	67 (24)	9 (3)	2 (1)	18 (6)	4 (2)	34 (12)
16.	U. Kannada	38 (14)	3 (1)	-	10 (4)	3 (1)	22 (8)
17.	Bellary	38 (15)	8 (3)	4 (2)	10 (5)	3 -	13 (5)
18.	Bidar	29 (11)	7 (3)	3 (1)	8 (3)	2 (1)	9 (3)
19.	Gulbarga	55 (19)	14 (5)	3 (1)	14 (4)	4 (2)	20 (7)
20.	Raichur	54 (19)	10 (4)	5 (2)	14 (5)	4 (1)	21 (7)
	Total	919 (335)	185 (63)	47 (22)	243 (89)	63 (19)	401 (142)

Note: Figures in brackets indicate seats reserved for women.

APPENDIX V

GOVERNMENT OF KARNATAKA
RURAL DEVELOPMENT AND PANCHAYATI RAJ SECRETARIAT

NOTIFICATION

No. RDP 5 ZPS 95 (i) Bangalore, dated, 13-1-1995

In exercise of the powers conferred by clause (2) of Section 2 of the Karnataka Panchayati Raj Act, 1993 (Karnataka Act 14 of 1993), the Government of Karnataka hereby classify and notify the following classes of citizens specified in the Annexure as backward classes for the purpose of reservation of seats and offices of chairpersons in Zilla Panchayat, Taluk Panchayat and Gram Panchayat, namely: Category A and Category B.

By Order and in the name of the Governor of Karnataka

PARVATHI KESHAVACHAR
Under Secretary to Government,
Rural Development and P-Raj Department

CATEGORY A

1.		Agamudi
2.	a.	Ambalakaran
	b.	Ambalakarma
3.		Bavandhi
4.	a	Bavaji
	b.	Atit
	c.	Bairagi
	d.	Bavani
	e.	Byragi
	f	Daurigosayi
	g	Davari
	h	Gosayi
	i	Gusai
	j	Helava
	k	Helova
	l	Holeval
	m	Nandiwala
	n	Nathapanthi
	o	Pichigunta
	p	Pichiguntala
	r	Bava
	s	Byaragi
5.	a	Bestha
	b	Ambiga
	c	Barki
	d	Besthar
	e	Bhoyi
	f	Bunde-Beshtar
	g	Daalji
	h	Daavat
	i	Gabit
	j	Galadakonkani
	k	Gangemakkalu
	l	Gangakula

	m	Gangamatha
	n	Gangamathastha
	o	Gangaputra
	p	Gowrimatha
	q	Bunde Bestha/Gunde Bestha
	r	Harakantha
	s	Jalagara
	t	Kabbera/Kabber
	u	Kabbaliga
	v	Kabbili
	w	Kahar
	x	Kharvi
	y	Koli
	z	Kolimahadev
	aa	Maddar
	ab	Meenagar
	ac	Mogaveera
	ad	Moger
	ae	Mukkavan
	af	Parivara
	ag	siviyar
	ah	Sunagara
	ai	Thoreya
6.	a	Bhamta
	b	Bhompta
	c	Paradeshi-Bhampta
	d	Takari
	e	Bhomptra
	f	Uchillian
7.		Bhatraju
8.	a	Bogad
	b	Begadi
	c	Bagali
	d	Bogadi
9.	a	Budubudukl
	b	Bududki
	c	Chhetri
	d	Devari
	e	Garadi
	f	Giddidki
	g	Joshi
	h	Kichagara
	i	Killikyata
	j	Modiga
	k	Pansa
	l	Panasa
	m	Pingalc
	n	Sadajoshi
	o	Budbudkala
10.		Chunchar
11.	a	Dasari
	b	Chakravadya-Dasa
	c	Dang-Dusur
	d	Dombi-Dasaru
12.	a	Devadasi
	b	Basavi
	c	Bhavin
	d	Bogam
	e	Ganika
	f	Kalavant
	g	Nat
	h	Natuva
	i	Patramela
13.	a	Ghisade
	b	Ghisadi
14.	a	Goniga Mane
	b	24 Mane Telugu Shetty
	c	Goni Chetty
	d	Sadusetty
	e	Salaparu
15.	a	Gurav
	b	Tamballa
	c	Tumbli
16.		Gurkha
17.	a	Halawakki Wakkal
	b	Halakki Vakkal
	c	Atte Vokkalu
	d	Gam Gawada
	e	Gam Vokkal
	f	Grama Vokkalu
	g	Halakki Vokkalu
	h	Kare Vokkalu
	i	Kunchavakkal
	j	Shilwakkal
	k	Vakkal
	l	Gavada
	m	Gam Gawda
	n	Gram Vakkal
18.	a	Hawadiga
	b	Hawgar
	c	Hooowgar
19.	a	Jogi
	b	Brahma Kapali
	c	Jogar
	d	Jogin

	e	Kapali
	f	Raval
	g	Ravalia
	h	Sanjogi
	i	Sanyasi
	j	Joger
20.	a	Kanjirbhat
	b	Kanjar
	c	Khanjar Bhat
21.	a	Kashikapadi
	b	Kashikapdi
	c	Tirumali
22	a	Katabar
	b	Katabu
23	a	Katik
	b	Aray
	c	Arc Kasai
	d	Ari Katikelu
	e	Kalal Khatik
	f	Kasab
	g	Kasai
	h	Maratti
	i	Suryavamsha Kshatriya
24.	a	Kolari
	b	Kalayiri
	c	Koleri
25	a	Kolla
	b	Kollala
26.		Kotari
27.		Kudubi
28.	a	Kurma
	b	Kurmi
29.	a	Ladaru/Ladara/Ladar
	b	Lad
	c	Yelegar
30.		Malaya
31.	a	Mccdara
	b	Batter
	c	Burned
	d	Gauriga
	e	Gouriga
	f	Gowri
	g	Gowrimaratha
	h	Gowriga
	i	Medari
	j	Burud
32.		Mudhar
33		Otari
34		Pamlor
35.	a	Pngual
	b	Pangusal
36.		Panika
37.	a	Raya Rawath
	b	Ravat
38.		Rcinudas
39		Sansia
40.		Satarkar
41.		Siddi
42.	a	Sikkaligara
	b	Shikalgar
	c	Shikkaligar
43.	a	Somavamsa Arya Kshatriya
	b	Chitara
	c	Chitragar
	d	Digwan
	e	Jeeragara
	f	Najabund
	h	Tambat
44.		Takankar
45.	a	Tewar
	b	Kalari
	c	Kallar
	d	Maravar
46.	a	Tilari
	b	Tirali
47.	a	Uppara
	b	Beldar
	c	Chunar
	d	Gavadi
	e	Goundi
	f	Kallu Kutiga Uppara
	g	Lonari
	h	Melu Sakkreyavaru
	i	Melusakkare
	j	Namada Uppara
	k	Padit/Padti
	l	Padithi
	m	Padi
	n	Sagara
	o	Sunnagara
	p	Sunna Uppara
	q	Uppaliga
	r	Uppaliga Shetty
	s	Uppaliyan
	t	Uppera

	u	Yakalara
	v	Yekkali
48.		Vidu
49.		Vasudev
50.	a	Veer
	b	Veeramasti
	c	Vir
51.		Yeralu
52.	a	Yerkala
	b	Erakala
	c	Kaikadi
	d	Koragar
	e	Kormasetty
	f	Kunchi
	g	Korwari
	h	Yrukala
53.	a	Bailpatar
	b	Bailapatar
	c	Bilapatar
54.	a	Bajania
	b	Bajenia
55		Balasanthoshi
56		Bazigar
57		DEria
58	a	Bhardi
	b	Bhargi
59	a	Chara
	b	Chhar
	c	Chhara
60.	a	Chapper Band (Muslim)
	b	Chapper Banda
61		Chitrakathijoshi
62		Darvesn
63		Dholi
64	a	Durgamurga
	b	Burburcha
65	a	Modikara
	b	Modikar
66	a	Gondali
	b	Ghondali
	c	Gondaliga
	d	Gondhali
	e	Gondhalli
67.		Vagri
68	a	Javeri
	b	Jawari
69.		Johari
70.	a	Kamatti
	b	Kaman
71	a	Kanjari
	b	Kanjir
72	a	Kalkari, Kclkari
	b	Khelkari
73	a	Kolhati
	b	Kolhatigi
74		Masania Yog'
75		Full Mali
76		Saraia
77	a	Sarordi
	b	Saroda
78		Vadi
79		Bedaru
80	a	Golla
	b	Yadav
	c	Asthanagolla
	d	Yadava
	e	Adavigolla
	f	Gopala
	g	Gopali
	h	Gouli
	i	Gauli
	j	Gavali
	k	Gavli
	l	Anubaru
	m	Hanabar
	o	Kavadi
	p	Kolayan
	q	Konar
	r	Konnur
	s	Krishna Golla
	t	Maniyani
	u	Urali
81	a	Banjari
	b	Brinjari
	c	Vanjara
	d	Wanjari
	e	Lambaid
	f	Gore or Goria
82.	a	Bendar
	b	Berad
	c	Boya
	d	Naikamakkalu
	e	Naikwadi
	f	Palegar
	g	Remoshi
	h	Talawar/ Talwar - Boya

	i	Valmikimakkalu
	j	Vedan
	k	Parivara Nayaka
	l	Myasa Nayaka
	m	Urs Nayaka
	n	Byada
	o	Haranshikari
	p	Chigari Betagar
	q	Vaghri
	r	Wagiri
	s	Nirshikari
	t	Bargi
	u	Baori
	v	Phasachari
	w	Hirshikari
83		Daveri
84	a	Garudi
	b	Garudiga
	c	Garadiga
85		Paradhis
86	a	Girni Waddar
	b	Tudug-Woddar
	c	Kallu Vaddar
	d	Mannu Voddar
	e	Bhandi Voddar
87	a	Bhoi
	b	Boyi
	c	Harikanthra
	d	Kharia
	e	Bovi
88		Pinjara
89		S.C. Converts to Christianity
90.	a	Agasa
	b	Chakala
	c	Dhobi
	d	Madivala
	e	Mannan
	f	Parit
	g	Rajaka
	h	Sakala
	i	Vannan
	j	Vclluthedan
	k	Sakalavadu
91.	a	Devadiga
	b	Devali
	c	Moyili
	d	Padiar
	e	Scregara
	f	Servegar
	g	Sheregar
	h	Suplig
92	a	Idiga
	b	Bandhari
	c	Belchad
	d	Billava
	e	Deevar
	f	Desha Bhandari
	g	Devar
	h	Devaramakkalu/Divara Makkalu
	i	Ediga
	j	Eliga
	k	Ezhava
	l	Gamalla
	m	Goundla
	n	halepaikaru
	o	Hale Paik
	p	Illavan
	q	Kalal
	r	Malayali Billava
	s	Nadar
	t	Namadhari
	u	Thiyan
	v	Iliga
	w	Goondla
	x	Tiyan
93.	a	Kumbara
	b	Chakrasali
	c	Gunaga
	d	Ganagi
	e	Koyava
	f	Kula
	g	Kulala
	h	Kumbar
	i	Kumbard
	j	Kummara
	k	Kusavan
	i	Moolya
	m	Sajjan Kumbara
	n	Khumara
	o	Kumbhar
	p	Khumbhar
	q	Kulalar
94	a	Kuruba
	b	Bharwad

	c	Dhanagar
	d	Goraya
	e	Halumatha
	f	Kurab
	g	Kuruban
	h	Kurumba
	i	Kurub
	j	Kurumban
95.	a	Nayinda
	b	Ambattan
	c	Bajanthui
	d	Bandari
	e	Chouriya
	f	Hadapada
	g	Hajama
	h	Kavutian
	i	Kelasi
	j	Kshaurika
	k	Kshowrad
	l	Mahale
	m	Manala
	n	Melagara
	o	Nadiga
	p	Napitha
	q	Navalig
	r	Navi
	s	Nayanaja Kshatriya
	t	Nhavi
	u	Savitha
	v	Nayanaja Kshatri
	w	Nadig
	x	Kshowrik
	y	Kshowrika
96		Buddhists
97	a	Tigala
	b	Agni Vamsha Kshatriya
	c	Agnivanni
	d	Agnikula Kshatriya
	e	Dharmaraja Kapu
	f	Palli
	g	Shambhukula Kshatriya
	h	Thigala
	i	Vanniar
	j	Vannikula Kshatriya
	k	Tigler
	l	Kurovan
98	a	Viswakarma
	b	Achari
	c	Akkasale
	d	Ausala
	e	Badigar
	f	Badiwadla
	g	Bailapatar
	h	Bailu Akkasali
	i	Bailu Kammara
	j	Bogara
	k	Chaptegar
	l	Charodi
	m	Daivgnya Brahmin
	n	Gejjara
	o	Kambar
	p	Kammalan
	q	Kammara
	r	Kamsala
	s	Kamsan
	t	Kanchagar
	u	Kanchora
	v	Kanchori
	w	Kanchugara
	x	Kansar
	y	Kasar
	z	Luhar
	aa	Mesta
	ab	Panchal
	ac	Pattar
	ad	Silpi
	ae	Sohagar
	af	Sonar
	ag	Sony
	ah	Sutar
	ai	Tacchan
	aj	Viswa Brahmin
	ak	Thattan
	al	Aksali
	am	Kamsal
	an	Badagi
99	a	Aghori
	b	Karkarmunda
100		Agnani
101		Ambalavasi
102		Anduran
103	a	Atari
	b	Athari
104		Bahurupi
		Bakadra
105	a	Bathal

	b	Battal
	c	Batter
106		Bawtar
107	a	Bhaat
	b	Bohrot
108		Binapatta
109		Bingi
110	a	Bagadi
	b	Bagaadi
	c	Bagdi
111	a	Chaliyan
	b	Teruvan
	c	Challiya
112		Chamboti
113		Chambukutti
114		Mestha
115		Jingar
116		Ghadi
117	a	Ghadsi
	b	Ghadshi
118		Pingle
119	a	Gosavi
	b	Gosain
120	a	Gujar
	b	Guzar
121	a	Gurava
	b	Gurou
122	a	Gabbit
	b	Gapit
	c	Gaabit
	d	Daalija
123	a	Marayan
	b	Hanabatti
124		Handevazir
125		Handervut
126		Honniyar
127	a	Hoovadiga
	b	Hugar
	c	Hoogar
	d	Maalgar
	e	Mali
	f	Phool Mali
	g	Phul Mali
	h	Phulari
	i	Phoolari
	j	jeer
128		Kadu Konkani
129		Karikudumbi
130		Karuva
131	a	Khatik
	b	Katuka
	c	Katuga
132.		Bogar
133		Kasbin
134	a	Kolayiri
	b	Kolyiri
135	a	Kanisan
	b	Kaniyar
	c	Kaniyaru
	d	Kaniya
	e	Kaniyan (other than Kollegal Tq. of Mysore District)
	f	Kanyan
136	a	Kanbi
	b	Kulwadi
	c	Kunbi
137		Kutuma
138		Marta
139	a	Marayan
	b	Maravan
140		Murrari
141	a	Nadora
	b	Uppu Nadar
	c	Torke Nador
	d	NAdor
	e	Nadavar
	f	Nadava
	g	Uppunador
142		Nalki
143		Osthan
144	a	Pandaram
	b	Pandar
	c	Pandara
145		Panaba
146		Pannckara Konkani
147		Patra
148		Pichati
149		Pullavan
150	a	Rajapuri
	b	Rajpur
	c	Balavalikar
151		Saniyaar
152		Shanan
153	a	Sudir
	b	Sudra

154 Sutsali
155 Tachayiri
156 Tilvi
157 a Gavandi
b Govandi
158 Vettuvan
159 a Yeklar
b Yaklar
c Egalika
160 a Gatti/Gattiyavaru
b Poledava/Poladavaru
161 Gudigara
162 a Darzi
b Bhavasar Kshatriya
c Chippi
d Chippiga
e Simpi
f Shimpi
g Sai
h Mirai
i Rangari
j Rangrez
k Nilari
l Namdev
m Namadev Simpi
n Rangare
o Neelagar
163 a Devanga
b Devang
c Koshti
d Hutgar/hutkar
e Jed
f Winkar
g Julohi
h Hulkar
i Hatagar
164. a Neygi
b Kuruhina Setty
c Bili Magga
d Thogata
e Soniga
f Jam Khana
g Ayiri
h Avir
i Sale
j Padma Sale
k Saale
l Kaikolan
m Neikar
n Jadar
o Jandra
p Sakula Sale
165. a Pategar
b Patvekari
c Pattegar
d Somavamsha
Sahasrarjuna Kshatriya
166 a Ganiga
b Teli
c Gandla
d Vaniyan
167 Rajput
168 Amma Kodava
169 Anappan
170 a Andi
b Andipandaram
171 Baandhi
172 a Balaballala
b Ballala
173 a Bhatial
b Bhattia
174 a Chakkan
175 Dogra
176 Gulli
177 Hindu Sadru / Sadaru
178 a Jaui, Jetty
b Mallaru
Malla Kshatriya
c Mushtiga
179 a Kalavanthi
b Bhogam/Teluga
180 a Kanakan
b Kanakar
181 a Kotegara
b Koteyar
c Kothati
d Kottegara
e Kotteyara
f Kumara Kshatriya
g Kumara Panth/
Komarpant
h Rama Kshatriya
i Rama Raj Kshatriya
j Serugara (North Kanara)
k Sergara (South Kanara)
l kote Kshatriya

182 a Kshatriya /Kshatri
183 Malawa
184 Maleya
185 Aryan
186 a Raju Kshatriya
b Raju - Raju
c Rajuwar/Rajavar/ Rachevar
187 Somavanisha Kshatriya
188 Stanika
189 a Tulu
b Tuluva
190 Muslim

CATEGORY - B

1. a Vokkaliga
b Vakkaliga
c Sarpa Vokkaliga
d Hallikar Vokkaliga
e Namdhari Vokkaliga
f Gangadkar Vokkaliga
g Das Vokkaliga
h Reddy Vokkaliga
i Marasu Vokkaliga
j Reddy
k Hallikar
l Kunchitiga
m Gouda
n Kapu
o Heggade
p Kamma
q Raddy
r Gownder
2. Kodagaru
3. a Balija
b Balajiga/Banajiga
c Naidu
d Bogam Teluga
e Telaga Balija
f Setty Balija
g Kasban
h Mannur-Munnar
i Mutrasi
j Maracha
k Janappan
l Balegara
m Banagara
4. a Veerashaiva Lingayath
b Lingayath Sub-groups of Helava, Ambiga, Bhoyi, Gangamatha, Sunagara, Agasa, Madivala, Kumbara, Kuruba, Bajanthri, Bandari, Hadapada, Kshaurika, Navalig, Navi, Akkasale, Badigar, Kammara, Kamsala, Panchal, Medar, Uppara
5 a Maratha/Marata
b Arekshatri, Are Maratha, Arya Maratha,
c Arya, Aryaru
d Konkan Maratha
e Kshatriaya Maratha
f Kulavadi
6 Christian
7 a Bunt/Bant
b Parivara Bant
8 Jains (Digambaras)
9 a Satani
b Chattada Srivaishnava
c Kudri Vaishnava
d Sameraya
e Sattadaval
f Sattadavan
g Vaishnava

Index

S

T

U

V

W

Z